TIME

Special Ops

TIME

MANAGING EDITOR Richard Stengel
DESIGN DIRECTOR D.W. Pine
DIRECTOR OF PHOTOGRAPHY Kira Pollack

SPECIAL OPS
The hidden world of America's toughest warriors

WRITER Jim Frederick
DESIGNER Arthur Hochstein
PHOTO EDITOR Dot McMahon
PHOTO RESEARCHER Lindsay Tyler
GRAPHICS EDITOR Lon Tweeten
CONTRIBUTORS James Poniewozik, Nate Rawlings
RESEARCHER Elizabeth L. Bland
EDITORIAL PRODUCTION Lionel P. Vargas

TIME HOME ENTERTAINMENT
PUBLISHER Richard Fraiman
VICE PRESIDENT, BUSINESS DEVELOPMENT AND STRATEGY Steven Sandonato
EXECUTIVE DIRECTOR, MARKETING SERVICES Carol Pittard
EXECUTIVE DIRECTOR, RETAIL AND SPECIAL SALES Tom Mifsud
EXECUTIVE DIRECTOR, NEW PRODUCT DEVELOPMENT Peter Harper
DIRECTOR, BOOKAZINE DEVELOPMENT AND MARKETING Laura Adam
PUBLISHING DIRECTOR Joy Butts
FINANCE DIRECTOR Glenn Buonocore
ASSISTANT GENERAL COUNSEL Helen Wan
ASSISTANT DIRECTOR SPECIAL SALES Ilene Schreider
BOOK PRODUCTION MANAGER Suzanne Janso
DESIGN AND PREPRESS MANAGER Anne-Michelle Gallero
BRAND MANAGER Michela Wilde

EDITORIAL DIRECTOR Stephen Koepp

SPECIAL THANKS TO:
Christine Austin, Jeremy Biloon, Jim Childs, Susan Chodakiewicz, Rose Cirrincione, Jacqueline Fitzgerald, Carrie Hertan, Christine Font, Jenna Goldberg, Lauren Hall, Malena Jones, Mona Li, Amy Mangus, Robert Marasco, Kimberly Marshall, Amy Migliaccio, Nina Mistry, Tara Rice, Dave Rozzelle, Adriana Tierno, Alex Voznesenskiy, Vanessa Wu, TIME Imaging

ISBN 10: 1-60320-244-7
ISBN 13: 978-1-60320-244-2
Library of Congress Control Number: 2011938113

We welcome your comments and suggestions about TIME Books. Please write to us at:
TIME Books, Attention: Book Editors, P.O. Box 11016, Des Moines, IA 50336-1016

If you would like to order any of our hardcover Collector's Edition books, please call us at 1-800-327-6388, Monday through Friday, 7 a.m. to 8 p.m., or Saturday, 7 a.m. to 6 p.m., Central Time.

Contents

Dedication

In death, as in life, special ops warriors almost always remain in shadow. A Pentagon press release might acknowledge their passing with no revelation of their true mission. The August 6 downing of a Chinook helicopter in Afghanistan was different. It was the first time in a war-filled decade that we learned about the lives of fallen special ops soldiers. Their loved ones told us who they were and why they were extraordinary, and we saw the faces of these men: 22 SEAL team members, five helicopter crewmen, and three Air Force special operators. (Eight Afghans also died.) Before this war is over, we will surely lose more from their ranks—and we should remember to honor their sacrifice, even if, unlike these heroes, we never learn their names.

TOP ROW (from left)
Matthew D. Mason, Jon T. Tumilson, Michael J. Strange, Robert J. Reeves, and Stephen M. Mills, Navy SEAL team members

SECOND ROW (from left)
Jason R. Workman, Heath M. Robinson, Nicholas P. Spehar, John Douangdara, and Aaron C. Vaughn, Navy SEAL team members

THIRD ROW (from left)
Jesse D. Pittman, Jared W. Day, John W. Faas, Kevin A. Houston, and Louis J. Langlais, Navy SEAL team members

FOURTH ROW (from left)
Kraig M. Vickers, Darrik C. Benson, Jonas B. Kelsall, Brian R. Bill, and Nicholas H. Null, Navy SEAL team members

FIFTH ROW (from left)
Thomas A. Ratzlaff and Christopher G. Campbell, Navy SEAL team members; Bryan J. Nichols, David R. Carter, and Daniel L. Zerbe; Army General Support Aviation Battalions

SIXTH ROW (from left)
John W. Brown and Spencer C. Duncan, Army General Support Aviation Battalions; Patrick D. Hamburger, Alexander J. Bennett, and Andrew W. Harvell, Air Force 24th Special Tactics Squadron

The Best And the Bravest

What it means to be one of America's elite warriors—and what their excellence means for the rest of us. By Bob Kerrey

FREE FALL
*High-altitude jumps allow U.S.
Air Force pararescue men to reach
difficult destinations in Afghanistan.*

After the successful assault of May 2, 2011, on the terrorist leader responsible for the 9/11 attacks, America's attention was focused on the skill and training of the U.S. Navy SEALs who executed the operation. Just three months later the attention shifted to the dangers of their work after 22 SEAL team mission members, five crewmen, and three Air Force special operations members were killed in a helicopter crash in Afghanistan. On Aug. 25, the Navy held a memorial service for their fallen.

Grieving done, their leaders were obliged to return to preparing themselves and their men for the next mission. Grieving done: That's the way it has to be. In civilian life grieving can go on indefinitely. For a SEAL it cannot. That may be the easiest way to understand the difference between them and us.

Every time I meet a member of our special operations forces, every time I think about their commitment to us, I ask myself the same question: Do Americans appreciate how lucky we are to have them serving us?

Those who choose to enter the ranks of special ops are a breed apart. I was once a Navy SEAL, but I do not pretend that my training 44 years ago to become one is equivalent to today's. Comparing the SEAL teams of 1967 and the SEAL teams of 2011 gives me the same feeling I get when I watch today's competitive swimmers. They dive into the water just as I used to do. The strokes and techniques look the same. But the results—the power, the speed, the stamina—are so different that I do not feel I have much in common with them.

Except for the butterflies both of us had in our stomachs before the gun sounded. Except for the need to embrace the pain that must be endured by all who choose to compete. Except for the commitment and sacrifice that separate those who get in the pool from those of us who don't.

Former Sen. Bob Kerrey as a Navy SEAL

We should be grateful that such people are willing to serve us in such dangerous, demanding ways.

Besides the famous missions in Pakistan and Afghanistan, thousands more never make headlines, since missions are carried out in secret. Yet they have become increasingly important to the U.S. in a world where small-scale acts of terrorism and unconventional warfare are the order of the day.

The attacks of 9/11 taught us that enemies of the U.S. who are determined to do us harm are not likely to look like former enemies. They won't be wearing uniforms, they won't be moving in large, easy-to-track formations, and they won't need highly sophisticated, expensive weapons. They will use our open communication, transportation, and financial systems to conduct their business. And they will live among people who are innocent of their intent and practices.

Special operations units must be prepared to go wherever the bad guys are. They must be able to locate and identify the enemy. They must be able to choose a range of weapons available to counter the threat. Day or night, they must be able to see, hear, and smell signs of danger. In all imaginable conditions, they must be skilled in aimed fire; they must be able to deliver a bullet to its intended target.

What enables our special ops units to achieve so much is their high standards in recruitment, motiva-

IN THE DARK
Most special operations missions, like this one in Afghanistan, take place at night.

tion, talent, training, and bravery. Valor alone does not guarantee success. Nor does training or talent. To do their jobs well, our special ops units need just as much know-how and courage from the civilians who lead them, or they would most assuredly fail. Americans may not be aware of it, but the politicians who write the laws overseeing our military, as well as civilians who help make the rules, have quietly revolutionized our armed forces in recent decades. A brief history might help.

In the beginning, there was an Army and a Navy, which became an Army, a Navy, a Marine Corps, an Air Force, and a Coast Guard. Each of the services has created its own specialized categories of work. That specialization has increased during the Information Age, in part because the military has been a leader in the development of communication technologies. The good news is that specialization allows a military group to do much more than if everyone had to be cross-trained in every skill. The bad news is that this specialization—and other factors—created walls that made it difficult for the services to collaborate. Inter-service rivalries dominated and detracted from the U.S. military's overall capabilities.

What changed all that was a law written by Sen. Barry Goldwater and Rep. William Flynt Nichols in 1986 to create joint forces. Now each regional commander has authority over the ground, air, and naval personnel and equipment that are needed to carry out his mission.

This is a big change from the past. Not even the demands of World War II produced real unity of command. The new "jointness" was applied to special ops as well, integrating these maverick units directly into the mainstream military. That change accelerated after President George W. Bush recruited Bob Gates to become Secretary of Defense and President Obama kept him onboard. Secretary Gates didn't have the Pentagon's old-fashioned territorial resistance to the intelligence community, in part because he was a former director of the CIA. The successful raid to get Osama bin Laden is a prime example of that new cooperation.

Command of special ops had to change too, which became painfully apparent after the failure of the 1980 Iran hostage rescue attempt. The units weren't cooperating, with tragic results. In a move that was resisted by the Pentagon, Sen. William Cohen and Sen. Sam Nunn, along with Rep. Dan Daniel, inserted a provision in the 1986 Defense Reform Law to create a major new arm of the military, a Special Operations Command, headed by a four-star general and its own assistant secretary of defense.

This gave special ops a voice at the highest level.

After having once operated at the margins of the military, the special ops warriors had become America's elite warriors. Yet being elite does not mean being arrogant. Just the opposite. Being elite imposes upon the individual the necessity for modesty, discretion, silence, and respect for every military and civilian person upon whom each mission's success depends.

Do Americans appreciate how lucky we are to have these special warriors serving us? This book should help readers get to the right answer.

Bob Kerrey, a former senator from Nebraska, received the Medal of Honor for his service as a Navy SEAL in Vietnam.

Warriors For the 21st Century

O N THE NIGHT OF MAY 1, 2011, two MH-60 Black Hawk helicopters, the workhorses of America's military, lifted off from Jalalabad Airport in eastern Afghanistan. But these were no ordinary helicopters, and this was no ordinary mission. These birds had been modified to increase their surveillance-evading capabilities—fitted with prosthetics to obscure their tell-tale radar profile and sheathed in a noise- and heat-dampening skin. Their extraordinary stealth was crucial because 15 minutes into their flight, the choppers slipped without permission into Pakistani airspace on a mission designed to get in and out of the country before the Pakistani military even knew they were there.

An hour and 15 minutes later, flying low and silent, the choppers bore down on a one-acre compound in Abbottabad, Pakistan, about a 75-mile drive north of Islamabad. At the controls of the Black Hawks were crews from the U.S. Army's 160th Special Operations Aviation Regiment, known by the nickname the "Night Stalkers." Their passengers: 23 commandos from the Naval Special Warfare Development Group, known to cognoscenti as DEVGRU, but by wider reputation as SEAL Team 6, one of the world's most effective and lethal combat units. Drawn from the military's most elite conventional units, they are trained more rigorously than any other to perform feats of outlandish bravery and risk-taking. While the existence of SEAL Team 6 is not quite the secret it used to be, we may never know the names of the men on

that night's mission. Not only was this essential to the security of the unit and their families, but SEAL Team 6 and America's other elite counterterrorism units live by a code of self-sacrifice and glory-avoidance that is almost fanatical. They are perfectly content that only their peers really know what they have achieved. This night's mission would make history.

While special ops raids like the Abbottabad assault had been taking place in Iraq and Afghanistan for more than a decade, this night's SEAL mission was extraordinary for two reasons—how deeply inside Pakistan it was taking place, and the target: Osama bin Laden. After nearly a decade of false starts and blind alleys, the members of an intra-agency task force believed they had finally located the head of al Qaeda by tracking the cellphone signals of one of his most trusted couriers to this unlikely location, a wealthy city heavily populated by the top brass of the Pakistani military, who had publicly vowed for years they were doing everything in their power to apprehend him.

The small team of CIA officers who had opened a surveillance office nearby found the daily habits of the residents at the Abbottabad compound so peculiar (the house had no Internet connection, residents burned their trash rather than had it collected, and the inhabitants tracked by the CIA would drive for 90 minutes before even putting batteries in their cellphones) that they became confident that the tall person they saw walking the courtyard for an hour or two every day— they dubbed him "the pacer"—was the long-sought mastermind of 9/11. President Obama, after receiving several briefings about the surveillance efforts and hearing debates about the attack plan, gave the assault its go-ahead on April 29. "I thought it was important," Obama said in a documentary on the History channel, "if we were going into a sovereign country, that we had to have some proof that it was actually bin Laden, rather than firing a missile into a compound." This was a job for America's deadliest unit.

The elite prepare themselves for things to go wrong, and this time something almost immediately did. Upon approach to the house in Abbottabad, one of the Black Hawks got sucked into its own rotor wash as it deflected off the high walls of the small compound. The chopper landed hard in the courtyard and was

A U.S. Navy SEAL prepares for a 2007 night mission near Fallujah; such missions allow special operations to take advantage of its night-vision superiority.

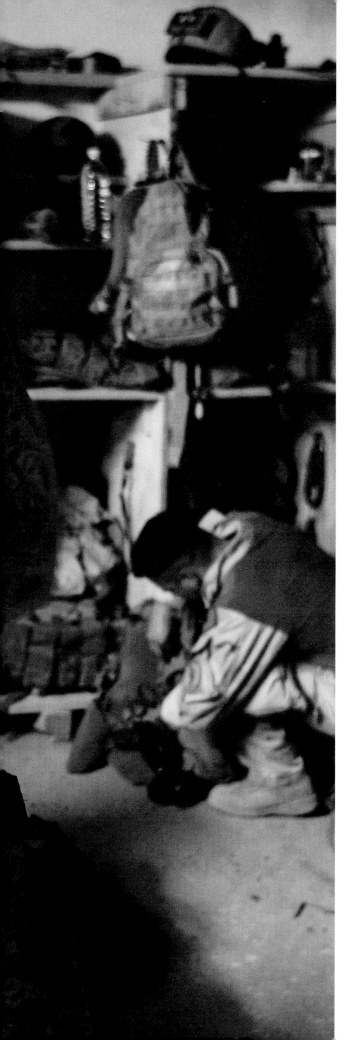

badly damaged. The other Black Hawk landed across the street. None of the SEALs aboard the first chopper were hurt, so the decision was made to "Charlie Mike," military phonetic slang for "Continue Mission." Most of the SEALs stormed the house, while a small contingent secured the perimeter. Accompanying the commandos were a Pakistani-American translator, who walked the front street pretending to be a local police officer, telling curious neighbors to return to their houses, and a highly trained military dog named Cairo.

The SEALs blasted through multiple metal gates as they stormed the house. In the guesthouse they saw the courier, who had just picked up a weapon. They shot him dead. Moving to the main house, they encountered the courier's brother and his wife. The brother was armed, the wife was not. The SEALs shot both dead. As they cleared the main house, they flushed bin Laden's 23-year-old son, Khalid, who was armed with an AK-47. They dispatched him too and moved to the third floor.

There they found their intended prey. Bin Laden, who had been codenamed "Crankshaft" for years, was standing behind two of his wives. Orders were to capture bin Laden only if he conspicuously surrendered, although a Pentagon official later said no one really thought that would happen. In the room, one SEAL tackled both women in one bear hug while another shot bin Laden first in the chest and then, as he fell back, above the left eye. The SEAL radioed the kill over an audio feed wired into the White House Situation Room, where President Obama, Secretary of State Hillary Clinton, and other key members of the President's national security team were listening and watching a grainy video feed from a drone circling 15,000 feet over the compound, waiting to hear the word "Geronimo," a mission-milestone codename to indicate that bin Laden had been found. "For God and country," said the SEAL, "Geronimo, Geronimo, Geronimo. Geronimo, E.K.I.A."—enemy killed in action.

The Americans suffered no casualties. After body-bagging bin Laden and combing the house for all the intelligence-laden hard drives and communications gear they could carry, they returned to the helicopters. The damaged Black Hawk was unable to take off, so the strike team decided to blow it up on the ground in an attempt to obliterate its technological secrets, and escape aboard the remaining Black Hawk and a Chinook transport helicopter that had been waiting in reserve. The helicopters slipped out of Pakistani airspace and back to Afghanistan. Bin Laden's body was the only casualty they carried back, and after doing DNA tests to verify they had the right man, a Navy team on the U.S.S. *Carl Vinson* conducted Islamic burial rites and buried him at sea. Total time the strike team spent on the ground: 38 minutes.

SEAL Team 6 reports to the Special Operations Command (SOCOM), the generals who control most of America's elite forces, including legendary units like Delta Force, more clandestine units like the Army's Intelligence Support Activity (often called just "the Activity"), as well as, most likely, several organizations that are still well-kept secrets. The killing of bin Laden—the way it was accomplished—is the best example yet of decades-long changes in how the U.S. military fights America's wars around the world.

Since the beginning of warfare, commanders have experimented with troops trained and deployed for special purposes. Over the centuries the term "special forces" has come to mean troops who are highly trained for specific, short-term missions, usually working in small numbers, typically in secret, often behind enemy lines, and designed to undermine a much larger force.

While elite squads played noteworthy roles in America's conflicts from the Revolutionary War to World War II, they fell into a marginal status during the Cold War era, when it was assumed that World War III was going to play out across the expanse of Europe, with U.S. and Soviet armor and infantry columns clashing in gigantic set-piece battles. In that environment special ops forces struggled for both funding and respect. Special ops might be appropriate for training guerrillas in the jungles of Asia or Latin America, but they were far from the center of military strategy, barely tolerated, and frequently distrusted by the top brass.

The rise of terrorism, especially after 9/11, changed all that. Special ops units have gone from small, renegade operations to being the core around which U.S. military strategy revolves. Special ops commanders are no longer at odds with the military establishment. Now

MEANWHILE, BACK HOME
The death of Osama bin Laden resonated all across the country, and in no place more than New York City.

they lead the establishment. And their commandos are better than ever at what they do. As President Obama said to the SEAL team that killed bin Laden, in a private meeting in which he was not told which SEAL fired the fatal shots, "You are, literally, the finest small fighting force that has ever existed in the world."

While many other parts of the military are coming under budget pressure, the ranks of special ops units have expanded to 61,000 soldiers and civilians, tripling in size since 9/11. Their missions have grown apace. In 2004, Defense Secretary Donald Rumsfeld signed an executive order empowering U.S. forces to hunt al Qaeda wherever it exists, regardless of other countries' borders. Under the Obama administration that mandate has only been amplified.

Despite the growth in their ranks, America's special ops warriors carry a heavy load, conducting missions in Iraq and Afghanistan, as well as in Yemen and Somalia and other locales that haven't been disclosed. At the Aspen Institute Security Forum in July 2011, Adm. Eric Olson, the outgoing chief of SOCOM, said that of the 33,000 troops scheduled to leave Afghanistan in the next year, not one of them will be a member of special ops.

Such a radical transformation in U.S. military strategy bears significant risks. Thousands of commandos are on secret missions, often without uniforms or battlefields, and when plans go wrong, they can go spectacularly wrong. In 2010, British aid worker Linda Norgrove was killed when U.S. Navy SEALs attempting to rescue her from captivity in Afghanistan threw a grenade too close to her. Moreover, special ops forces operate in a world of murky legality and ethics that can be perplexing. The bin Laden mission touched off a controversy on several fronts: Pakistan was outraged that its airspace had been so flagrantly violated. And several commentators wondered whether it was befitting of America's professed high moral standards to have highly trained troops operating essentially as hit squads.

Yet the enemies these troops face can be committed, tenacious, and unrelenting. Three months after the bin Laden raid, a Taliban fighter in Afghanistan downed a Chinook helicopter with a single rocket-propelled grenade, killing all 38 onboard, including 22 members of a SEAL Team 6 mission. Days later the loss became the backdrop for the swearing-in of SOCOM's new chief, Adm. William McRaven, the second Navy SEAL to hold the top post, at a ceremony at SOCOM's headquarters at MacDill Air Force Base in Tampa. "We will never forget your sacrifice nor the ultimate price your loved ones paid," said McRaven, "protecting us from those who would do us harm." The Taliban who shot down the Chinook helicopter eluded U.S. forces for just days before he was killed by an F-16 air strike.

SEAL's Rogue Commander

The founding commander of SEAL Team 6, Richard Marcinko was a polarizing figure who made no apologies for the enemies he killed in Vietnam—or the enemies he made throughout the U.S. military. But that kind of bombast doesn't rate in today's special operations community, which emphasizes quiet professionalism above all. Most SEALs express gratitude to Marcinko as the founding father of the elite unit, but they stress it is a different organization today. After serving 15 months in prison for defrauding the government by steering business to contractors in which he was a silent partner, Marcinko has launched a successful second act as the CEO of a security consulting company and the author of the Rogue Warrior series of military novels and nonfiction leadership books.

The Killing of Osama bin Laden

Abbottabad, Pakistan, 2011

The Mission

After almost 10 years of searching for the architect of 9/11, U.S. intelligence agents tracked him down through his courier's cellphone. The compound was monitored for several months before President Obama approved an assault, without informing the Pakistani government. Carried in by specially equipped, stealthy helicopters on the moonless night of May 1, commandos from SEAL Team 6 killed bin Laden and hauled away his corpse after only 38 minutes on the ground.

The compound was situated in a town full of Pakistani military elite.

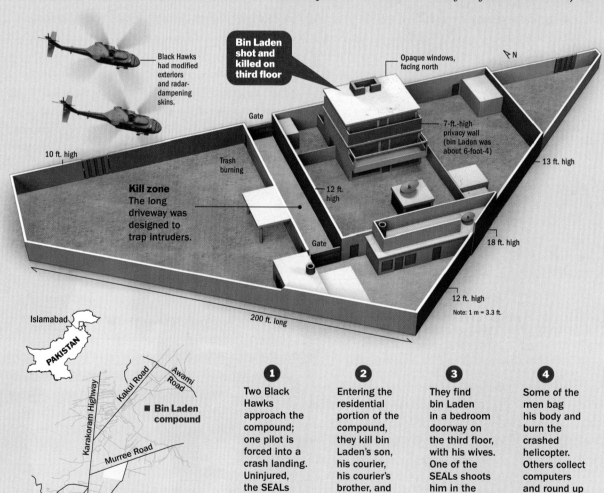

Black Hawks had modified exteriors and radar-dampening skins.

Bin Laden shot and killed on third floor

Opaque windows, facing north

N

Gate

7-ft.-high privacy wall (bin Laden was about 6-foot-4)

10 ft. high

13 ft. high

Trash burning

Kill zone The long driveway was designed to trap intruders.

12 ft. high

Gate

18 ft. high

12 ft. high

Note: 1 m = 3.3 ft.

200 ft. long

Islamabad

PAKISTAN

Karakoram Highway

Kakul Road

Awami Road

Murree Road

■ Bin Laden compound

ABBOTTABAD

1 mile
1 km

1 Two Black Hawks approach the compound; one pilot is forced into a crash landing. Uninjured, the SEALs assume their positions.

2 Entering the residential portion of the compound, they kill bin Laden's son, his courier, his courier's brother, and the brother's wife.

3 They find bin Laden in a bedroom doorway on the third floor, with his wives. One of the SEALs shoots him in the chest and forehead.

4 Some of the men bag his body and burn the crashed helicopter. Others collect computers and round up the remaining occupants.

The President's national security team gathered to watch a video of the mission from a drone overhead.

An aerial view of the compound, at the end of a dirt road.

Commandos burned the stealth chopper to obscure its secrets.

The house, which will be razed, has fortified concrete walls.

Bin Laden's third-floor bedroom; he was shot in the doorway.

CHAPTER 2

The Making of a Commando

MARCUS LUTTRELL was about 12 years old when he realized, almost inevitably, that he wanted to be a Navy SEAL. He was growing up in Texas on his parents' horse-breeding ranch, where his father made sure his sons mastered all the masculine arts of horsemanship, swimming, and shooting. Luttrell's father had been a Navy gunner in Vietnam, and he regaled his sons with tales of a new breed of warrior that came into its own during that war: commandos called SEALs because they were capable of amazing feats in the sea, air, and land. As Luttrell says in his book, *Lone Survivor*, which chronicles not just his training but an ill-fated 2003 SEAL Team 10 mission in Afghanistan, "In his opinion they were all that is best in the American male—courage, patriotism, strength, determination, refusal to accept defeat, brains, expertise in all they did."

Luttrell knew he wanted to be a part of that world. But first he would have to make the cut. "The work is brutally hard, the fitness regimes are as harsh and uncompromising as any program in the free world," Luttrell wrote. "The examinations are searching and difficult. Nothing but the highest possible standard is acceptable." To him the sacrifices were worth it. "When someone tells you he is in the SEAL teams, it means he has passed every test, been accepted by some of the hardest taskmasters in the military," he wrote. "When someone tells you he's in a SEAL team, you know you are in the presence of a very special cat."

Members of America's most elite squads—among them the Rangers, Special Forces, Force Recon Marines, and Air Force Special Tactics Squadrons—can all

UPHILL ALL THE WAY
During the mountain phase of training in Ranger School, soldiers prepare to climb up and rappel down a 50-foot rock near Dahlonega, Ga.

SAND AND SEA
In Coronado, Calif., potential SEALs must pass an intensive course that includes long runs through the sand and rigorous swimming tests with their hands tied behind their backs.

rightfully make such lofty claims. Special ops troops are the most highly trained warriors in the world. Most such units accept only a tiny fraction of those who try out. And once accepted, a special ops soldier has only begun a career of constant and rigorous training. While selection and training regimens vary among units—many claim that theirs is the most demanding of all—membership in any special ops force requires a level of physical and mental toughness not seen in virtually any other walk of life.

In applying for the military's most rarefied special ops units, it helps to come up from a service that's rigorous in its own right. The 75th Ranger Regiment specializes in difficult offensive strikes; one of its primary roles is to serve as backup for many Delta Force, SEAL Team 6, and other black-ops missions. Rangers face an exceedingly strict selection and training process, which makes their ranks a popular candidate pool for the top tier of special ops.

Besides completing all basic and advanced individual training and airborne school, soldiers hoping to become Rangers must score in the 60th percentile or better in the Army's standard physical fitness test (perfect score for pushups: 71 in two minutes). Beyond that, entrance requirements include being able to finish a five-mile run in 40 minutes or less, complete a protracted road march with a heavy pack, navigate a wide-ranging swimming test, pass a full psychological-profile screening, and qualify for a U.S. government security clearance at the "secret" level.

After that, applicants take a pre-Ranger course in which they hone their fitness and weapons skills further before the real test begins: Ranger School. The school is a 61-day immersion and simulation course designed to test and train small-group leadership and assault tactics (everyone in a class is stripped of rank, and everyone takes turns leading) with three increasingly intense phases in mountain, forest, and swamp settings.

The course severely restricts caloric intake and sleep. Instructors design scenarios to induce maximum stress and confusion. Sgt. First Class Floyd Getchell, who was the honors graduate of his 1986 Ranger class, says, "I was 155 pounds when I went in and 123 when I graduated. But mostly it pushed me mentally. That's the whole key of the special ops community: Under their guidance, they'll show you what you are capable of psychologically." Less than 50% of the men who start Ranger School graduate, which earns them the right to wear the small yellow-and-black Ranger tab on the left sleeve of their uniform for the rest of their career.

Another renowned Army unit, the Green Berets, has a similarly fearsome screening process, which includes the Special Forces Qualification Course (known as the "Q Course"), which, depending on assignment, lasts from 56 to 95 weeks. It begins with long, exhausting physical-fitness tests and marches and a land navigation test. The most notorious phase is SERE, which stands for Survival, Evasion, Resistance, and Escape, a brutal exercise that sends soldiers out into the woods alone without food or water to be hunted down by trainers acting as an enemy force. Candidates are inevitably captured and then subjected to four days of being treated like a prisoner of war.

An almost mystical code of silence surrounds this phase: Few, if any, Green Berets have ever spoken of what takes place during this training, but Maj. Rusty Bradley, who wrote a book about his experiences called *Lions of Kandahar*, gives a sense of it: "It's not just physical toughness, it's mental toughness. You might get put on a road or down a trail that might encompass two to three counties and two to three states. You need to know how to ration your own food and water. You're given a small piece of information, and it's simply, How do you manage yourself and how hard do you push yourself? They want to see how in-

HELL WEEK
In this phase of SEAL training, candidates undergo relentless exercise and the stress of loud noises and sleep deprivation.

novative you are. Obviously your physical prowess is going to be brought into question every day. They do an analysis of your strengths and weaknesses, and you have to be able to recognize them and be open-minded enough to use them. It doesn't just make you physically tired; it makes you mentally tired. It sucks and it's fun."

Other Green Beret requirements include multiple outdoor training exercises, including a 40-mile trek with a fully loaded rucksack and a simulation in which Q Course teams are expected to link up and form an alliance with a band of instructors playing a guerrilla army from the fictional republic of Pineland. It's often a humiliating and frustrating exercise—just as such operations can be in real life. As the only U.S. military unit with a language requirement, Special Forces candidates spend a major portion of their Q Course in classrooms learning one of scores of languages and dialects.

For all SEALs, the basic entry test after a three-week indoctrination course is a 25-week ordeal called Basic Underwater Demolition/SEAL. To qualify for BUD/S, seamen have to prove extraordinary fitness on land and in the water. Minimum benchmarks to qualify include a 500-yard swim in 12.5 minutes, 42 pushups in two minutes, 50 sit-ups in two minutes, pull-ups, and a 1.5-mile run in boots and pants in 11.5 minutes—all with no more than 10 minutes' rest between events.

The course focuses intensively on the uniquely maritime aspects of the SEALs' mission: underwater combat, underwater demolition, and attacking an enemy vessel at sea. The course begins with 10 weeks of intensive orientation and conditioning. Miles of running and hundreds of pushups a day are just the beginning. Water exercises are intense, designed not just to increase fitness and proficiency but to also test for panic at the point of exhaustion. Among the ex-

ercises: bobbing up and down to the bottom of the pool 20 times, floating for five minutes, swimming to the shallow end of the pool without touching the bottom and swimming back to the deep end, doing forward and backward somersaults underwater, and retrieving a face mask from the bottom of the pool with your teeth—all with your arms tied behind your back. Says Howard Wasdin, author of the bestselling *SEAL Team Six*, about his special ops experiences: "BUD/S does a good job of weeding out who will and who won't quit, and that's what BUD/S is designed to do. You see the guys that, no matter how bad it gets, they're going to keep coming."

This phase culminates in the famous Hell Week, which subjects candidates to stressful harassment exercises involving high-decibel noise exposure, sleep deprivation, and temperature extremes as they cycle though a nearly endless circuit of calisthenics, running, and pool and ocean exercises in freezing-cold water well beyond the threshold of mild hypothermia and hallucinations.

After that follows a combat diving phase (including underwater navigation and combat), a land warfare phase (weapons, marksmanship, explosives, land navigation, and rappelling), SEAL qualification (cold-weather combat, advanced paramedic training, and SERE), and finally airborne-school training in both static-line and free-fall parachuting. Completing all of that, candidates finally receive their trident insignia and are assigned to a SEAL team. Of the 180 applicants who started SEAL training with Marcus Luttrell, only 35 graduated.

Not to be outdone, Air Force Pararescue Jumpers spend two years in training, during which they complete the following schools: Pararescue/Combat Con-trol Indoctrination Course, Airborne School, Combat Diver School, Underwater Egress Training, Basic Survival School, Freefall Parachute School, Combat Medic Course, and Pararescue Recovery Specialist School.

For the most elite units of all, like SEAL Team 6 and Delta Force, having passed one or more of those indoctrinations is just the beginning. The selection and training processes for these units are much more closely held secrets, but some details do leak out. Members of regular SEAL teams can submit an application to join SEAL Team 6 throughout the year, and applicants are interviewed intermittently. Those selected from the interviews are given a date to report for what is called Green Team, the SEAL Team 6 selection and training unit. While on Green Team, candidates undergo intense training: One former member estimates he did about 150 parachute jumps in four weeks. Candidates are also subjected to more SERE training: free climbing, unarmed combat, defensive and offensive driving, boatcraft, and obstacle courses. Instructors grade and rank the candidates' every move.

At the end of the six-month Green Team training (the dropout rate is said to be 90%), those chosen to join SEAL Team 6 are selected by the unit's permanent teams in a round-robin process that's like a professional sports league's draft. Scouts from each of the teams (Red, Blue, Gold, and Grey) take turns picking from the graduating Green Team class, looking for those with the skills they're most in need of.

While even less is known about Delta's selection course, it's believed to reflect the earliest selection tests devised by Delta Force founder Charlie Beckwith. Delta Force operators are recruited throughout the Army, sometimes through tryouts, but most often they are pulled from Special Forces and Ranger units. Like SEAL Team 6, a member of Delta will interview the person interested and often give them an on-the-spot fitness test before they are asked to join the selection process.

Candidates chosen for Delta selection then undergo what's believed to be a month-long selection process (known in the community as "tryouts"), involving an initial fitness test followed by long treks in the wilderness. Candidates are given a map and compass, told the grid coordinates of a location called a Rendezvous Point, and instructed to get there as fast as they can without using roads or trails. Crucial for the Delta mentality, candidates are not told the cutoff time they need to beat, which disturbs a lot of longtime Army folks, who spent their entire careers knowing exactly how fast they needed to accomplish a test in order to pass. Candidates are likewise never given any feedback about their performance throughout the process. Delta's selection thus carries with it the vestiges of the SAS's heavy emphasis on psychology and mental maturity in the face of the deeply difficult moral dilemmas a modern warrior faces.

The phase ends with a 40-mile task with no time standard and no guidance other than to "do your best and move as hard as you can." But with each checkpoint believed to be the last, candidates are given one more; the instructors are looking for those who will become frustrated and quit. According to Eric Haney, a former Delta operator and author of *Inside Delta Force*, what can seem like psychological tricks serve a higher purpose. "They are looking for a good sense of judgment, a comprehension of a larger picture. And tenacity and confidence." Finally, after most candidates have given up hope that the checkpoints will ever end, they are given the word: "Congratulations, you made it. It's over."

After selection, Delta candidates go through a six-month program called the Operators Training Course. This course focuses on intensive weapons training, not just on a shooting range, but with an emphasis on close-quarters combat—shooting while running and meticulously picking off enemy targets who may be only feet if not inches from a hostage or innocent bystander. Other training includes assault techniques custom-tailored for airplanes, ships, trains, and cargo trucks.

The training philosophies of both SEAL Team 6 and Delta Force are rooted in a similar respect for the operators' own maturity and intelligence to self-direct his own training. There is none of the rote, soldierly discipline chores found in the regular Army. No one insists on boots being shined unless there is a good reason that they have to be shined. No one has to insist that an operator's weapons are clean: It's assumed that they always are. Special ops units take pride in how much training autonomy they enjoy. Says Haney: "Everything was based on our mission forecast. Why waste valuable training time with things you're not going to do? That was the largest thing over any conventional unit we had going for us: We focused on our missions and the tasks that the men needed to be able to perform to accomplish those missions." And at the moment of truth, no one can doubt their readiness.

ONLY THE BEGINNING
This soldier had a 12-mile march before taking a cour to qualify for Ranger Schoo

How the SEALs Trained Me For Life

Zinke in Iraq, where he was deputy commander of special ops

Ryan Zinke, a former member of SEAL Team 6, was elected to the Montana state senate in 2009. He talked about his 23-year career as a SEAL with Time's Nate Rawlings.

I don't come from a military family, but after I played football in college, a former admiral asked me what I was going to do. He said, "If you are looking for a very tough, team-oriented career, you should consider something in the SEALs."

I was both a student and an instructor at Basic Underwater Demolition/SEAL. It is far more humorous on the instructor side. Each of the activities—what we call evolutions—has a purpose. As a student, you don't see the purpose; you just see that it's very painful. There's often no beginning, and you don't know when it's going to end. The only control you have is staying or leaving. Hell week is generally in the fifth week, and there is very little preparation you can do other than not quit.

Everyone is going to be wet. Everyone is going to be miserable. The water is going to be cold. It's easy to think about getting out of the water and going someplace warm. It's a lot harder to think about staying there and just getting colder, but that's the expectation of a SEAL.

At SEAL Team 1, we were doing cold-weather operations in the Aleutian Chain. We were in the North Sea with 20-foot waves, surrounded by pods of killer whales. You're going in at night on a beach when the surf is 20 to 30 feet, then across islands that were in the middle of a blizzard. You start out wet, and everything you own is soaked; then you go inland, and you're a walking icicle. Everything is frozen. I grew up in Montana, where it's cold. I've never been that cold.

I both sought, and was sought out, to interview and go through the selection process for SEAL Team 6. You have to be able to filter and make decisions very quickly. They deal with hostage rescues, weapons of mass destruction—those types of no-fail missions—so you have to be able to shoot, move, and communicate at a faster level. I was on that team for eight years, and I was gone, on average, 220 days a year. After SEAL Team 6, I served as part of a joint coalition in Bosnia, where we found and brought to justice a number of individuals who were convicted of heinous war crimes. There was a sense of satisfaction doing those types of operations in a war that brought out both the best and worst of mankind.

After 9/11, I went forward as the deputy commander of Special Operations in Iraq. We were doing two or three operations a night somewhere. The last mission I was on, I jumped out of a helicopter and stepped in a hole, and I was kind of hobbling up to where the SEALs were standing. I heard one of them say, "Hey, the old man's here." And I looked around, and I said, "We need to clean this place up. The old man's here." I started looking for the old man; then it dawned on me that they were talking about me.

The SEALs run pretty fast. They run hard. There is a point where you really can't be operational on target and that was the point for me. I spent 23 years in, helped my nation, and figured I'd use some of that leadership expertise to help my state. So I went back, ran for office, and won. People expect results, so I'm working really hard to gain some ground. The SEALs look at a problem, look at the available assets, prioritize the assets, then charter a mission to fix the problem. We need to roll up our sleeves and do the SEAL mission, which is fix things.

Picking Off the Somali Pirates

Indian Ocean, 2009

YEMEN
Gulf of Aden

ETHIOPIA
SOMALIA

● Eyl

Somali pirates killed by sniper fire

AFRICA

KENYA

☆ Mogadishu

Indian Ocean

The Mission

While some missions are planned for months, others are in response to emergencies, like the successful rescue of the captain of a U.S. merchant ship taken in a wave of modern-day pirate attacks off the Horn of Africa. It was reported to be the first hijacking of a U.S. ship since 1821.

On April 8, 2009, four Somali pirates who had hijacked a Taiwanese fishing vessel two days earlier used a skiff from that boat to board the M.V. *Maersk Alabama*, a U.S. cargo ship with a crew of 20 en route to Mombasa, Kenya.

As the pirates boarded, the crew disabled the ship's systems, then hid, but the pirates took Captain Richard Phillips hostage.

The crew members, who had received anti-piracy training, were able to regain control of the ship when chief engineer Mike Perry tackled the ringleader and took him hostage. A hostage swap went wrong when the Somalis failed to honor their side of the deal, and they fled to one of the ship's lifeboats with several days of food and Captain Phillips in tow.

The next day the destroyer U.S.S. *Bainbridge* arrived and established communication with the pirates; two more U.S. ships followed. As the weather worsened, the pirates agreed to allow the lifeboat to be towed to Mombasa, and one pirate came aboard the *Bainbridge* to negotiate a ransom.

On April 12, after one of the pirates was seen holding an AK-47 to the back of Captain Phillips, the captain of the *Bainbridge* decided Phillips' life was in danger and ordered direct action. Three SEAL snipers, who had parachuted into the water near a Navy ship two days earlier, positioned themselves on the fantail and fired on the three remaining hijackers simultaneously, killing them all. Captain Phillips was taken aboard the *Bainbridge* unhurt. The hijacker on the ship, Abduhl Wali-i-Musi, was taken into custody and transported to the U.S., where he was found guilty of piracy and sentenced to more than 33 years in prison. Since that episode there have been several more attempts by pirates to hijack the *Maersk Alabama*, none successful.

U.S. Navy SEALs, like this one aiming from a helicopter, are some of the sharpest shooters on earth.

From top left: A team from the U.S.S. Boxer tows the lifeboat from the Maersk Alabama, where the pirates had held Capt. Richard Phillips; Phillips several months after his rescue; one of the four pirates, Abduhl Wali-i-Musi, who surrendered and survived; the Maersk Alabama, berthed in the Kenyan port of Mombasa at the time of the standoff.

The Special Ops Hall of Fame

F THERE IS A LEGEND THAT EMBODIES THE core values of special ops, it is Herodotus' account of the Battle of Thermopylae (in 480 B.C.), describing a last stand by 300 Spartans and their Greek allies in a narrow pass against an invading force of Persians numbering in the thousands. Their resistance to King Xerxes' army has long been used to instill the principles of elite warriors: skill, loyalty, sacrifice, and a willingness to face overwhelming odds. Compared with other Greek soldiers, Spartans were the special ops of their day, undergoing punishing exercise regimes and rigorous training in weapons and tactics.

While much military history dwells on the epic movements of battleships and army divisions, the David vs. Goliath tales of special ops offer their own surprising narratives. "A successful special operation defies conventional wisdom by using a small force to defeat a much larger or well-entrenched opponent," wrote Adm. William McRaven, now the chief of U.S. Special Operations Command, in his 1995 book, *Spec Ops*. McRaven focused his case studies on commandos of the 20th century, but heroic examples go back to ancient times. In the First Punic War (264–241 B.C.), Hamilcar Barca, who was charged with commanding the Carthaginian land forces against the Romans in Sicily, extended the losing conflict by using a small number of specially trained troops to create havoc and confusion among his foes. For three years he ran several operations every day, harassing Roman troops with guerrilla tactics, frustrating the much larger traditional army. Hamilcar's better-known son Hannibal kept up the family tradition during the Second Punic War (218–

THE LAST STAND
The 300 Spartans and their Greek allies fought thousands of Persians in the battle of Thermopylae.

202 B.C.), again employing surprising and wily tactics to keep Roman troops almost constantly off guard.

A millennium later, after the First Crusade ended in 1099, the Knights Templar, which began as nine monks charged with protecting Christian pilgrims in Jerusalem, gradually expanded their duties over the next two centuries to mount a broader defense of the crusader states. They became the advance force in key battles, a role that many special ops forces play today. The Templars' most effective tactic was a furious mounted charge in an attempt to break opposition lines. One of their most celebrated victories was the Battle of Montgisard in 1177, where 500 Templars helped defeat Saladin's army of 26,000 soldiers.

The ninja of feudal Japan were trained to infiltrate, sabotage, spy, and assassinate, although they could participate in conventional open combat as well. Unlike the more ritualistic and straightforward samurai, ninja clans were secret. They practiced the martial art of ninjutsu, the art of stealth. Ninjutsu closely resembled jujitsu in its use of an opponent's energy against himself, but adapted to the need for evading enemy samurai. Ninja weapons were made to resemble the threshing tools of Japanese farmers so that they could be easily concealed. They studied scouting and the use of poisons and explosives, trained in long-distance running, and learned about common professions in order to pass in disguise.

In the New World, battle tactics employed by Native Americans became crucial to Western militaries. During the French and Indian War (1754–63), Maj. Robert Rogers of Maine led an independent company of 600 militia attached to the British Army. They successfully adopted many Native American techniques, including camouflage, stealth, small-unit independence, and a raiding attack style. The tactics employed by Rogers' Rangers were so effective that by the late 1750s the unit had become the chief scouting unit of the British forces.

After the Revolutionary War the U.S. Army realized the benefits of specialized troops who could take advantage of the increasing accuracy and decreasing load times of the rifle. In 1808 the First Regiment of U.S. Riflemen was organized, borrowing heavily from Native American ways. They were masters of conceal-

ment and were frequently sent ahead of the main attacking force to observe and disrupt enemy movement and snipe enemy officers.

During the Civil War, the mention of John Singleton Mosby, known as the Gray Ghost, and his unit, called Mosby's Rangers, would strike fear in the heart of Union soldiers. His small squad of about 60 men operated behind enemy lines in northern Virginia, an area that became known as Mosby's Confederacy. The Rangers' mission was, he said, "to weaken the armies invading Virginia by harassing their rear." When a scout found a target of opportunity, Mosby would gather his group. With the enemy surrounded, the Rangers descended upon the objective and struck swiftly. The element of surprise was paramount: "A small force moving with celerity and threatening many points on a line can neutralize a hundred times its own number," Mosby declared.

SPECIAL ANCESTORS: *Clockwise, from top left: A Knight Templar during the Crusades, as shown in an 1847 illustration; a Japanese ninja making a secret finger sign; a group of Mosby's Rangers during the Civil War; Francis Marion, considered to be a father of guerrilla warfare, leading his troops in South Carolina during the Revolutionary War*

With the proliferation of communications and transport technologies since World War I, any nation that hoped to win a war needed a concerted spy effort. In 1941, Franklin Roosevelt appointed William "Wild Bill" Donovan to run a U.S. intelligence department that would come to be known as the Office of Strategic Services (OSS). Donovan's OSS was, according to CIA historian Thomas Troy, "a novel attempt in American history to organize research, intelligence, propaganda, subversion, and commando operations as a unified and essential feature of modern warfare; a 'Fourth Arm' of the military services." The OSS racked up several notable successes during the war: recruiting German diplomat Fritz Kolbe, training troops in China and Burma to support resistance throughout Southeast Asia, and helping to create the "Jedburgh teams" that parachuted into France in 1944 to support the D-Day invasion of Normandy. Although the OSS was shut down af-

ter the war, it was effectively restarted in 1947 with a new name: the Central Intelligence Agency. As with its precursor, the CIA's sometimes functional, sometimes utterly dysfunctional relationship with U.S. military intelligence and special ops units would remain one of its defining characteristics well into the 21st century.

On the battlefields of World War II, U.S. Army Rangers, with their small-unit raiding style, came into their own. The first World War II ranger group was known as Darby's Rangers. Of the 1,500 servicemen who volunteered to serve under Maj. William Orlando Darby, only 600 were chosen. Their successful invasions in North Africa in November 1942 opened the Mediterranean Sea and its ports for the Allied forces, an early and decisive victory upon which the entire European campaign relied. In the Pacific a comparable group known as Merrill's Marauders was charged with disrupting Japanese communication and supply channels behind enemy lines in Burma. For five months in 1943–44, Marauders traveled more than 1,000 miles and participated in 35 successful engagements without armor or artillery support, including the capture of the only all-weather airstrip in Burma.

As the Cold War began, Maj. Gen. Robert Mc-Clure and others in the military realized that the U.S. and the Soviet Union would increasingly be vying for domination via proxy wars across the world with smaller countries and revolutionaries acting under the influence of the superpowers. Founded in 1952, the Army's Special Forces were all volunteers, trained to infiltrate deep into enemy territory. They were airborne-qualified, proficient in languages, trained in sabotage and psychological operations. They specialized in organizing and training and fielding militias. Their motto was "*De Oppresso Liber*"—to free the oppressed—and originally they were called the "10th Special Forces Group" in the hope that the Soviet Union would think there were nine more of them.

It was during the Vietnam war, however, that Special Forces came into its own as the U.S. Army's unconventional-warfare specialists. Numbering only a few thousand, Special Forces teamed up with South Vietnamese troops and civilian tribesmen to form irregular militias like the Montagnards to wage harass-

ing insurrections against the Viet Cong.

During this period they became known by the metonymic moniker stemming from their distinctive headgear: the Green Berets. The beret dated from World War II, when British commandos who drilled U.S. Rangers and OSS officers would award them a beret at the completion of their training. Ever since then, U.S. graduates of British commando courses would wear them as badges of honor, but it always had to be on the sly since they were not an approved uniform item in the U.S. military. But President John F. Kennedy was interested in the mission of Special Forces, seeing them as a powerful weapon against the spread of communism, so in 1961 he authorized the official wearing of the beret. The bond between the President and the unit was so strong that Special Forces soldiers were among the honor guard at his funeral; one trooper left his beret on Kennedy's coffin.

For decades the Green Berets were one of the only true special ops units the U.S. had. It was certainly the best known, thanks to the 1965 bestselling book *The Green Berets* by Robin Moore and the 1968 John Wayne movie of the same name that was loosely based on it. Never mind that the movie is poorly done (the *New York Times* called it "full of its own caricature of patriotism" and "out of touch"), the real unit logged several landmark engagements in Vietnam, including bloody action during the Tet offensive.

After a period of lavish and excessive bravado

(tiger-skin capes, elephant-skin boots), the Green Berets retrenched psychologically and philosophically, pioneering an ethos of anonymity and avoidance of the spotlight that pervades most special ops forces to this day. The Green Berets began cultivating a community of a highly selective, highly elite meritocracy. Green Beret soldiers, especially because of the attention brought upon them by Hollywood, became culturally averse to seeking any public glory whatsoever.

A rule of thumb became that anyone who claimed in public to have been a Green Beret probably hadn't been. This sort of fame aversion has only intensified with more recent and deep-cover units.

One of the defining characteristics of a Special Forces unit is how it is organized. Each company generally consists of six ODAs (Operational Detachments-A) or A-Teams, with each ODA focusing on a particular specialty such as urban operations, underwater diving and demolition, high-altitude paratrooping, or mountain warfare. An ODA typically consists of 12 men, each of whom also has a specific specialty, such as medicine, engineering, communications, or intelligence. With two men to each specialty, the A-Team can also split up into two six-man teams. Every Special Forces soldier is given basic training in every subject area to ensure some redundancy. From its genesis, Special Forces has put a premium on local language skills.

The Green Beret qualification course (or Q-Course) is a punishing multiweek physical and mental endurance test mimicked or improved upon by virtually every spec ops unit since. What the Green Berets and other special ops units struggled to overcome was a reputation among the military's top leadership as undisciplined, unaccountable, and out of control.

(Col. Robert Rheault, head of all Special Forces in Vietnam, was one of the inspirations for the renegade Col. Kurtz in *Apocalypse Now*.) In an Army oral-history project in 1973, former Army chief of staff Harold K. Johnson said that the Green Berets in Vietnam were "fugitives from responsibility. These were people that somehow or other tended to be nonconformists, couldn't get along in a straight military system, and found a haven where their actions were not scrutinized too carefully, and where they came under only sporadic or intermittent observation from the regular chain of command." The culture clash was so deep that many Green Berets took Johnson's comments as a compliment. As a sign of how far the Army has come since then, its recruiting slogan from 2001–06 was "An Army of One," a theme of independence unthinkable to earlier generations of infantry grunts.

THE GREEN BERET
Capt. Vernon Gillespie Jr. wearing the potent symbol, borrowed from British tradition, at a firing range in Vietnam in 1964

Military Tactics on the Home Front

On August 21, 1991, 32 Cuban immigrants who were jailed at the Talladega Federal Correctional Institution in Alabama took over the prison's maximum-security unit. They took nine hostages and demanded a stay of their deportation order back to Cuba. Negotiations broke down, and the acting U.S. Attorney General gave the order to assault the prison.

At 3:43 a.m., members of the FBI's Hostage Rescue Team (HRT) blew doors open with explosives, tossed flashbang and concussion grenades, then stormed the building. The HRT agents rushed to the hostages while members of FBI SWAT teams forced more than 120 prisoners back into their cells. The entire assault was over in three minutes; the agents didn't fire a shot.

While most counter-terror units operate under extreme secrecy, the FBI's HRT openly acknowledges its role as a unit capable of military direct action in support of local police. The rise of terrorism in the 1970s showed the need

The FBI's hostage-rescue teams play many roles, including this patrol in response to Hurricane Katrina in 2005.

for a domestic commando unit like Delta Force. After witnessing a Delta exercise in 1981, FBI director William Webster asked why the Delta operators didn't carry handcuffs. The Joint Special Operations commander replied, "It's not our job to arrest people." Since federal law generally prohibits the military from operating on domestic soil, Webster decided to assemble a unit that could carry out the tactical actions of commandos but also arrest suspects, investigate crime scenes, and testify before grand juries. The unit went into operation

in 1983. While it suffered from mistakes and controversy in the standoffs at Ruby Ridge and Waco, it has handled more than 850 hostage-rescue and other missions since it was founded.

Today the HRT has nearly 500 members. FBI agents with five years of experience can try out for the HRT at FBI headquarters in Quantico, Va. The standards are similar to military special ops units: The candidates must pass a fitness test with sit-ups, pushups, pull-ups, a 1.5-mile run, and a 300-meter sprint. Those selected undergo a six-month training

course at the HRT's small compound in the U.S. Marine Corps Base at Quantico. Trainees have to navigate the Tactical Firearms Training Center, where they practice assaults in a mockup of an airplane, a multistory tower, and other lifelike situations. Every part of the center has embedded cameras and microphones so the instructors can break down a trainee's performance much like a football coach after practice. Right next door is the HRT's tactical helicopter unit, where trainees fast-rope from helicopters and learn the elements of speed, surprise, and precision shooting. They reportedly blast, ram, and kick through 30 doors a day and fire thousands of rounds a week.

HRT members train regularly with Navy SEALs, Delta Force, and the Coast Guard as their role expands beyond the U.S. Since 9/11, agents have conducted six-month deployments to Iraq and Afghanistan, as well as shared their expertise with European police agencies.
—*Nate Rawlings*

The Father Of Delta Force

FEW INSTITUTIONS ARE AS TRA-dition-bound as the military, which is why its visionaries are often seen as renegades in their day. Gen. Billy Mitchell, now considered the father of the U.S. Air Force, was even court-martialed for insubordination. If special ops has a comparable figure, it is Col. Charlie Beckwith, the creator of the U.S. Army's secret unit known as Delta Force. A career officer who had served in the Korean conflict, Beckwith became obsessed with the idea of creating an elite unit after training as an exchange officer with the Special Air Service (SAS), Britain's legendary commando unit. He deployed with them in 1962 to fight the communist insurgency in Malaya, where he became convinced that the U.S. military desperately needed a special ops unit that could do what the SAS did: fight terrorists and insurgents in small units with an extremely low profile. The U.S. military at that point had the U.S. Special Forces, also known as the Green Berets, who excelled at teaching foreign militias and armies how to conduct unconventional warfare. But Special Forces were not focused on hunting and killing these enemies themselves. And that was a problem. The U.S. Army, Beckwith wrote, needed a unit "to be able to go out in small patrols and blow up bridges and dams and railroad lines, to take out an enemy commander." The American Army needed "not only a force of teachers but a force of doers."

On his return to the U.S., Beckwith wrote a report recommending the creation of an SAS-like unit. No one paid any attention to it. Beckwith, who had played football at the University of Geor-

CHARGIN' CHARLIE
Beckwith declared that the Army needed "not only a force of teachers but a force of doers."

What We Learned From the British

Although the U.S. now fields the most fearsome array of commando units on the planet, they weren't the first of their kind. America's special ops pay unreserved homage to the group that pioneered this style of fighting, served as the inspiration for the first U.S. counterterrorism units, and remains among the most lethal black ops forces around: Britain's Special Air Service (SAS).

The SAS can trace its roots to the deepest days of World War II, when Lt. David Stirling hit upon an idea to put the new technology of parachuting to work in a novel way. What if a small group of commandos dropped far into enemy territory and employed extreme stealth and evasion while wreaking havoc on supply lines, enemy installations, and other ripe targets? Over the next four years the SAS launched dozens of successful such missions across Europe and Africa.

It was after World War II, however, as Britain tried to keep

This heavily armed SAS group had just returned from a three-month patrol in North Africa during World War II.

hold of its increasingly restive empire, that the SAS evolved from an outstanding raiding troop into the pioneering masters of counterinsurgency and counterterrorism. During the Malayan Emergency the SAS was instrumental in helping native Malayan troops and citizens resist a communist revolution attempt. Living and working among the locals for long periods, the commandos became masters at reconnaissance, jungle combat, and psychological warfare. SAS members trained local militias, but they also did much

of the hunting down and killing of terrorists themselves, while placing priority on winning the hearts and minds of civilians—a combination that serves as a model for counterinsurgency in practice to this day.

The SAS excelled in small-unit tactics—a four-man unit was the basic building block—which allowed them to be very quick and flexible. Small group size also helped them achieve another priority: an extremely low profile. SAS units did not shy away from using civilian clothing, disguises, lock picking, and other

clandestine tradecraft to achieve their aims.

In the 1950s and '60s, the SAS developed a culture that has set the tone for special ops forces worldwide. Call it an understated excellence. The SAS demanded that its men maintain the very highest standards but also remain as inconspicuous as possible. And it accepted only the best of the best. One could not just join the SAS, unlike other army units; the distinctive unit beret had to be earned through a punishing qualifying course that evaluated mental toughness as much as physical endurance. Over the decades since, the SAS has been deployed to every major military engagement Britain has been involved in—and many missions that have never been publicly acknowledged.

America's special ops and the SAS have cooperated closely. Especially during the wars in Iraq and Afghanistan, wherever Delta Force, SEAL Team 6, or the Army Rangers were, odds are an SAS squadron was nearby.

gia and had turned down an offer from the Green Bay Packers in order to join the Army, demonstrated all the stubbornness of his college team's mascot, a bulldog. Discouraged but undaunted, Beckwith became an operations officer with the 7th Special Forces Group. There he found troops who were supposedly masters of unconventional warfare but surprisingly inept at basic soldiering. Before a Green Beret could be a good "unconventional soldier," Beckwith wrote, "he'd first have to become a good conventional one." He overhauled Green Beret training, dramatically increasing instruction and drills and intensifying the difficulty of the qualifying course. (Later he'd do the same with U.S. Army Ranger training.) Assigned to Vietnam, he took command of a secret Special Forces program known as Project Delta, which, with the help of South Vietnamese special forces, mounted long-range reconnaissance missions deep into enemy territory.

In 1977, as terrorist attacks and hijackings became more and more high profile, Beckwith got the go-ahead to set up a unit along the lines he had proposed earlier. The name he chose: 1st Special Forces Operational Detachment—Delta. Beckwith had estimated that it would take 24 months to get his new unit mission-ready, and fate delivered him almost exactly that amount of time. On Nov. 4, 1979, Iranian revolutionaries stormed the U.S. embassy in Tehran, taking 66 Americans hostage. Initially Beckwith didn't believe a rescue attempt would be Delta Force's first big mission; it looked to him like folly. "Logistically speaking," he wrote in his memoirs, "it would be a bear. There were the vast distances, nearly 1,000 miles of Iranian wasteland, then the assault itself, against a heavily guarded building complex stuck in the middle of a city of 4,000,000 hostile folks. ... Nothing could be more difficult."

Nonetheless, Delta began preparing for the mission, and as diplomatic resolutions kept breaking down, Beckwith's unit ultimately got the call. Delta Force was ordered to carry out Operation Eagle Claw, a plan to covertly enter the country and recover the hostages from the embassy during what was supposed to be a two-day mission, starting April 24,

BY SEA, AIR, AND LAND
The U.S. Navy SEALs were established in 1962 after the Bay of Pigs fiasco, but have roots in World War II groups.

1980. The plan was ambitious and complex, calling for eight Sea Stallion helicopters (flown by Marine Corps pilots) and six transport planes (flown by Air Force pilots) to rendezvous at a refueling point at a remote desert locale deep inside Iran. The helicopters were then to fly the Delta troopers to a hideaway near Tehran, where they would lie low for a day before being transported by trucks driven by other Pentagon operatives. At that point, Delta would storm the embassy, free the hostages, get picked up and ferried to another runway via the helicopters, and then be flown out of the country. Even the Delta members were daunted by the long odds of this mission. During their early days of training, they had always assumed that their base of operations would be a friendly country. Said one Delta operator: "The difference between this and the Alamo is that Davy Crockett didn't have to fight his way in."

Indeed, it was a disastrous failure (see box at the end of this chapter). The mission never got past the first stage. After three of the helicopters developed mechanical problems—at least two of them because they encountered a devastating sandstorm—Beckwith, with the approval of President Carter, aborted the mission. But as the assault force was preparing to evacuate, disaster struck. A hovering helicopter clipped one of the planes, setting off a ferocious explosion that killed eight men and destroyed both aircraft.

It was an embarrassing failure for an already humiliated nation. Beckwith was blamed and publicly castigated. In the *New York Times*, William Safire opined, "Col. Beckwith implies that he did the right thing. He did not; his disastrous decision should be examined by future military leaders at our war and naval colleges as a prime example of an excess of prudence in combat.... Adm. Farragut's 'Damn the torpedoes' has been replaced by Colonel Beckwith's 'We gotta go back.'"

Even though he was soon moved to a new unit, his career effectively over, Beckwith remained defiant, insisting that the mission's failure was an indication that the U.S. military was not taking his vision seriously. Beckwith's own assessment maintained that Delta was just the start of what needed to be

NEW WORLD, NEW WARFARE
Protesters burn a flag at the U.S. embassy in Iran in November 1979 soon after taking hostages.

a far more comprehensive special ops program. "In Iran, we had an ad hoc affair," he wrote. "We went out, found bits and pieces, people and equipment, brought them together occasionally, and then asked them to perform a highly complex mission.... My recommendation is to put together an organization which contains everything it will ever need, an organization that would include Delta, Rangers, Navy SEALs, Air Force pilots, its own staff, its own support people, its own aircraft and helicopters. Make this organization a permanent military unit." Informally Beckwith often put his philosophy in saltier terms: "I'd rather go down the river with seven studs than with a hundred shitheads."

A military panel reviewing the fiasco, the Holloway Commission, affirmed many of Beckwith's opinions. Among the deficiencies: an inadequate number of backup helicopters, lack of training among the Marine pilots for desert flying, and little warning about bad weather. Overall, however, those were symptoms of a bigger problem: the lack of centralized authority to oversee training, planning, coordination, and control between special ops units from every branch of the military that might be called upon to work together.

The Holloway Commission also recommended the creation of a permanent Counterterrorist Joint Task Force, an idea that ultimately became the Joint Special Operations Command (JSOC), the military's combined headquarters for America's top antiterrorism units. Among those units now under its command are the Navy's SEAL Team 6, which was founded in 1980 as the Navy's answer to Delta Force, and the Air Force's 24th Special Tactics Squadron, as well as other related units.

A TERRIBLE WAY TO LEARN A LESSON
A helicopter collided with a refueling plane, killing eight servicemen after the hostage rescue mission had been aborted.

As the fallout from Eagle Claw continued, two events in October 1983 further demonstrated the need for change: The terrorist bombing in Lebanon that killed 241 U.S. servicemen, plus more special ops mishaps during the U.S. invasion of Grenada (four SEAL Team 6 members drowned and 15 other servicemen were also killed) reinforced lawmakers' conviction that the military needed to be better integrated. In 1986, Congress passed the Goldwater-Nichols act, a momentous change in military structure that created a unified command for special operations, the U.S. Special Operations Command (SOCOM).

The moves confirmed the Reagan administration's clear desire to bolster the role of special ops forces in America's broader military strategy. In 1987, Reagan set a target to increase special ops forces by 50% from 1981 levels. Presidents Bush and Clinton continued the trend. Throughout the 1980s and 1990s, special ops participated in dozens of missions around the globe, largely under the radar, throughout Latin America and the Middle East, including tracking down Colombian drug lord Pablo Escobar, apprehending Serbian war criminals like Stevan Todorovic, and aiding mujahadeen fighters against the Soviets. One particularly public defeat, however, was Operation Gothic Serpent, a special ops mission to apprehend two associates of a Somalian drug lord in Mogadishu. Although the mission was a success, many Americans thought the price was too high: 18 U.S. troops killed.

Despite that tragedy, special operations had undergone a renaissance. However, 9/11 would push it to the very forefront of U.S. military strategy.

Six Secrets Of Success

Special ops warriors are known for their toughness, but there is an intellectual basis for their work too. Adm. William H. McRaven, who now commands all U.S. special ops forces, wrote a book, Spec Ops (1995), in which he identified six essential principles of successful missions. McRaven, the commander of SEAL Team 3 at the time, made case studies of eight legendary raids of the 20th century and discovered how small forces can achieve relative superiority over much larger ones:

SIMPLICITY: Planners need to limit the number of objectives, gather intelligence to reduce the number of unknown factors, and use innovative technology to overcome complications. When U.S. Special Forces attacked a North Vietnamese POW camp in 1970, they used commercially available low-light scopes to increase their shooting accuracy in the dark to 95%, up from 35%.

SECURITY: The team preparing for the mission needs to be secretive about its plans to avoid giving the enemy any sense of the timing or method of the attack. When a German unit was getting ready to raid a Belgian fortress at the beginning of World War II, the detachment was renamed and moved frequently; soldiers weren't allowed to send mail or make calls without approval. Recalled one sergeant: "Once we ran into some girls we knew, and the whole unit had to be transferred."

REPETITION: Full dress rehearsals are necessary. "The plan that sounded simple on paper must now be put to the test," writes McRaven, who quotes a British crewman who served on a midget-sub attack on a German battleship in 1943: "If you are going to do anything dangerous, the best way to accomplish it is to train, train, train, so that in the excitement of the situation you do the thing automatically."

SURPRISE: It's likely that any worthy target is going to be prepared for an attack, but a special ops force can catch an enemy off-guard through "deception, timing, and taking advantage of the enemy's vulnerabilities," writes McRaven. A German team that rescued Italian dictator Benito Mussolini from a mountain stronghold attacked precisely at 2 p.m., knowing that "the Italian guards would have just finished lunch and would be resting afterward."

SPEED: When attacking a superior force, special ops troops will have only a small window of time before the enemy mounts a counterattack. In McRaven's study, "relative superiority" was typically achieved in five minutes, and the missions completed in 30 minutes. In the raid on Osama bin Laden's compound, SEAL Team 6 members were on the ground only 38 minutes.

PURPOSE: Individual soldiers need to thoroughly understand the primary objective, and they need to have "a dedication that knows no limitations," wrote McRaven. "In an age of high technology and Jedi knights, we often overlook the need for personal involvement, but we do so at our own risk."

A Hostage Rescue Leads to Disaster

Iran, 1980

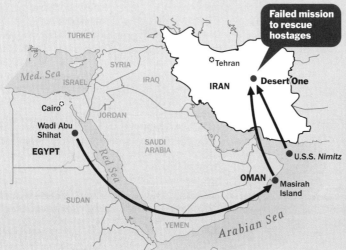

Failed mission to rescue hostages

The Mission

Soon after radicals took over the U.S. embassy in Tehran and captured 66 hostages, President Carter ordered military planners to draw up rescue scenarios. The failure of the complex Operation Eagle Claw led to a reorganization of the U.S. military and the rise of special ops.

PHASE 1: Eight RH-53D Sea Stallion helicopters were to fly from the U.S.S. *Nimitz* aircraft carrier in the Indian Ocean to a site known as Desert One in the Iranian desert. There they would rendezvous with MC-130E Hercules transport planes coming from Egypt via Oman's Masirah Island. Three carried fuel. One carried Delta Force commandos. This was the only phase completed successfully.

PHASE 2: The Sea Stallion helicopters were to fly the Delta Force soldiers to Desert Two, a concealed site just outside Tehran, where they were to offload the commandos. From there, the CIA planned to secretly transport the troops to the embassy in trucks.

PHASE 3: The CIA would then cut the electricity to the area, and the U.S. troops would overpower the Iranian soldiers guarding the U.S. embassy.

PHASE 4: U.S. troops would escort the hostages to the Shahid Shiroudi Stadium, where the Sea Stallion helicopters would pick them up.

PHASE 5: The Sea Stallions would transport the hostages to Iran's Manza-riyeh Air Base, outside Tehran. By that point, a squad of Army Rangers was to have taken over the air base and allowed C-141 transport planes to land. They would have transported the Delta Force and hostages out of Iran under the protection of fighter jets.

Disaster

The mission was aborted after its first phase. A sandstorm known as a *haboob* forced fine desert sand straight up thousands of feet, where it hung like a vertical cloud for hours, wreaking havoc on the helicopters. Of the eight Sea Stallions that left the *Nimitz*, two were damaged in the sand storm (one returned to the *Nimitz*, the other crash-landed). Another made it to the Desert One site, but incurred hydraulics damage and could not continue.

The mission called for a minimum of six helicopters to carry out the raid on Tehran. With only five functioning helicopters, Delta Force leader Col. Charlie Beckwith recommended aborting the mission. President Carter agreed.

As the five undam-aged helicopters refueled for their trip back to the

Nimitz, one crashed into a Hercules transport plane and exploded, killing eight soldiers and burning many more. Ammunition aboard both aircraft began exploding and damaged the remaining aircraft.

As time and fuel ran low, all the helicopter crews transferred to the two remaining Hercules planes and departed the area (leaving all remaining helicopters on Iranian soil).

Aftermath

The investigating Holloway Commission named 23 issues that contributed to Eagle Claw's failure. They included:
✔ Inadequate number of backup helicopters
✔ Navy and Marine Corps helicopter crewmen not well trained for this type of flying
✔ Poor training for inclement weather
✔ Inadequate weather forecasting

✔ Lack of a comprehensive, full-scale training exercise (the scene of Desert One was chaotic even before the accident)
✔ Ad hoc organization and lack of coordination among the multiservice commanders
✔ Security measures had serious downside consequences (the final plan was never committed to paper, so no one, including the Joint Chiefs, could properly study it)

Odd details: At the supposedly deserted Desert One site, the first landing party encountered two Iranian trucks, which fled. Rangers blew up one; the other got away. A bus with 40 passengers also appeared. Detained, they were to be flown out, but after the crash occurred, orders were given to evacuate immediately. Soldiers disabled the bus and released the passengers to go their own way.

The Mavericks Take Over

THE FIRST TIME MOST AMERIcans heard the name Stanley McChrystal was in mid-2009, when President Obama promoted him to four-star general and commander of U.S. and allied forces in Afghanistan. The appointment took many in Washington by surprise too: Stanley who? McChrystal was not a man accustomed to the schmoozing rituals of the Beltway. But national security cognoscenti knew exactly who he was: a killer. Having just completed a five-year stint as the chief of Joint Special Operations Command (JSOC), which oversees America's most secret military units, like SEAL Team 6 and Delta Force, Stan McChrystal was the quintessential black-ops war-

rior. McChrystal was one of a new generation of military leaders who became top commanders in the post-9/11 era and completed the transition from a military run by Cold Warriors like Norman Schwarzkopf, Tommy Franks, and Colin Powell to one focused on terrorism and the so-called small wars that prevail today.

A West Point graduate, McChrystal did several tours with the Army Rangers and developed a reputation as a kind of warrior monk, getting by on only one meal and a few hours of sleep a day. He was known as an aggressive soldier unafraid of the moral ambiguities of black ops, yet also a scholar who had put in stints at Harvard and the Council on Foreign Relations. During his 2003–08 tenure at JSOC, McChrystal forged better ties with the CIA and other intelligence units, leading to several successes like the capture of Saddam Hussein in 2003 and the killing of Abu Musab al-Zarqawi, the leader of al Qaeda in Iraq, in 2006. Under McChrystal, JSOC became a terrorist-hunting operation conducting thousands of missions and ratcheting up its proficiency and lethality. But controversy followed McChrystal as well. Thirty-four members of one JSOC task force were disciplined in 2004 for prisoner abuse at Abu Ghraib. McChrystal and his coterie were so accustomed to operating in the shadows that it eventually undermined his career. He was forced to resign in 2010, after *Rolling Stone* quoted members of his staff making disparaging remarks about the President and Vice President.

THE CATALYST
As defense chief, Rumsfeld pushed for smaller, faster fighting units.

McChrystal's departure had little to do with policy differences. In fact, Obama had surprised many by not only maintaining his predecessor's focus on special ops but intensifying it. In 2009, Obama named Vice Adm. William McRaven as McChrystal's successor to head JSOC, the first Navy SEAL to run the command. Under McRaven, JSOC has expanded its activities even further beyond the battlefields of Afghanistan and Iraq, including a deal with Yemeni President Ali Abdullah Saleh to conduct clandestine operations with Yemeni troops against al Qaeda in the Arabian Peninsula. But McRaven dedicated most of his attention to Afghanistan. On his watch U.S. special

ops forces killed or captured hundreds of Taliban and terrorist leaders, primarily in the new style of rapid-fire, unrelenting nighttime raids. The raids, sometimes numbering more than a dozen a night, have been one of the cornerstones of the Afghan war strategy. "Nobody thought it would be possible, frankly, to take that command beyond what Stan McChrystal did, but he has," Michael G. Vickers, undersecretary of defense for intelligence, told the *Washington Post.* "He has taken what was already a very integrated interagency organization and taken it to another level." In April, Obama promoted him to head the U.S. Special Operations Command, which oversees not only JSOC but more conventional special ops units like the Green Berets and Army Rangers.

The May 2 raid on Osama bin Laden's compound, which followed McRaven's promotion by three weeks, was the crowning achievement of JSOC to date. But the high-profile mission has brought more fame and attention to these units than they ever wanted. Despite the huge dividends that JSOC's methods have paid over the past few years, the risks are huge as well. The persistence of nighttime raids has strained relations with the Afghan government, which says that the raids often kill innocent civilians and that the U.S. is not held accountable for its mistakes. As McChrystal told *Washington Post* reporters, "Sometimes our actions were counterproductive. We would say, 'We need to go in and kill this guy,' but just the effects of our kinetic action did something negative and [regular Army forces] were left to clean up the mess." Yet the proven success of what JSOC calls its "unblinking eye" and willingness to hunt terrorists wherever they are will be a cornerstone of American security policy for the foreseeable future. As virtually the entire U.S. military is facing budget cuts, and several sacred cows are being examined, no one is talking about touching JSOC's $1 billion budget or the ranks of 4,000 service members and civilians now under its command. McChrystal and McRaven owe their rise to one, perhaps surprising, person and his vision for the future of U.S. mili-

The Chain Of Command

U.S. Special Operations Command (SOCOM)
Commander: Adm. William H. McRaven
MacDill Air Force Base, Tampa

28,500 troops	16,000 troops	8,800 troops	4,000 (estimate)	2,600 troops

Army Special Operations Command
Fort Bragg, N.C.

John F. Kennedy Special Warfare Center and School

Trains soldiers in 41 courses to enter the Army's special ops.

Special Forces Command

Also known as the Green Berets, they deploy worldwide to train and fight with foreign forces.

● 1st Special Forces Group

● 3rd Special Forces Group

● 5th Special Forces Group

● 7th Special Forces Group

● 10th Special Forces Group

Groups divided over Asia Pacific, Middle East, Central and South America, and Europe.

75th Ranger Regiment

Three battalions specializing in raids and forcible entry.

160th Special Operations Aviation Regiment

Known as the Night Stalkers, they fly choppers to infiltrate and exfiltrate special ops troops.

Air Force Special Operations Command
Hurlburt Field, Fla.

23rd Air Force

Provides close air support and reconnaissance for special ops forces in all branches. Planes carry Gatling guns, 40mm and 105mm cannons.

● 1st Special Operations Wing

● 27th Special Operations Wing

● 352nd Special Operations Group

● 720th Special Operations Group

Combat controllers coordinate air strikes; pararescue men retrieve downed pilots and operators.

Naval Special Warfare Command
Naval Base Coronado, Calif.

Naval Special Warfare Group 1

● SEAL Teams 1, 3, 5, 7

Conduct direct-action missions from Coronado, Calif.

Naval Special Warfare Group 2

● SEAL Teams 2, 4, 8, 10

Conduct direct-action missions from Little Creek, Va.

Naval Special Warfare Group 3

● SEAL Delivery Vehicle Team 1

Deliver SEALs to the battlefield with modified submarines

Naval Special Warfare Group 4

Three special boat teams conduct coastal patrols.

Joint Special Operations Command
Fort Bragg, N.C.

Officially a coordinating group, JSOC is also known to command the most elite and secretive special ops. It has grown rapidly since 9/11 and specializes in such missions as counterterrorism, lightning raids, hostage rescue, and covert operations.

● Naval Special Warfare Development Group (also known as Seal Team 6 or DEVGRU)

● 1st Special Forces Operational Detachment Delta (also known as Delta Force)

● Air Force 24th Special Tactics Squadron

● Intelligence Support Activity (a supersecret unit sometimes called "the Activity")

Marine Corps Forces Special Operations Command
Camp Lejeune, N.C.

The Marine Special Operations Regiment

● 1st Marine Special Operations Battalion

● 2nd Marine Special Operations Battalion

● 3rd Marine Special Operations Battalion

Organized into 14-man teams that operate anywhere for extended periods with minimal support.

Marine Special Operations Support Group

Includes teams that control firepower from ships and planes.

Marine Special Operations Intelligence Battalion

Provides intelligence support.

SEARCH AND DESTROY
As head of Afghan operations,
McChrystal (second from left) stepped
up nighttime raids in Afghanistan.

tary forces: Donald Rumsfeld. When he arrived at the Pentagon in early 2001 as President Bush's Defense Secretary, a number of prominent generals and civilian policy thinkers were already agitating for change. The U.S. military was, they charged, too big, too slow, and too focused on preparing for a World War III in which massive infantry and armor battles would rage across entire continents. This mindset persisted even though the Soviet Union had disintegrated nearly a decade earlier and China was still decades away from being able to muster that kind of strength. The military, reformers contended, was woefully ill-equipped to fight the small, tenacious terrorist groups who wore no uniforms and held no territory.

Rumsfeld, who had long subscribed to this belief, now had the power to launch some of the most sweeping changes the U.S. military had ever seen. He pushed Pentagon brass to make the U.S. military lighter, smaller, more agile, and more technologically sophisticated. He completed an initiative begun in the 2000s to make the U.S. Army's primary deployment unit not the division (comprising anywhere from 10,000 to 20,000 troops) but the brigade (typically 3,000 to 4,000). This type of modular, quick-pivot organization would make it easier to send troops anywhere in the world at a moment's notice, with less logistical and material support.

In Rumsfeld's grand plan, special ops held a particularly privileged position. Despite their being lionized in movies and pop culture, special ops had never held a lofty position in the Pentagon's pecking order. Mainstream generals may have tolerated them, but their unconventional ways were unnerving to most top commanders, and few bothered to really understand the commandos they called "snake eaters," let alone figure out how best to use them. They operated by night, they worked alone, and they acted like renegades, which is inimical to some of the bedrock virtues that most military men hold dear.

To Rumsfeld, special ops exuded the very qualities with which he wanted to infuse the entire military. After 9/11, his views on this point only hardened. In a world where terrorists lurk in the cave warrens of Afghanistan and the crowded streets of Sanaa, Yemen, Rumsfeld believed, handfuls of fast-moving men could seek and destroy pinpointed targets more effectively than could thousands of conventional troops. In late 2001, as the Bush administration prepared for a counterattack against al Qaeda and the Taliban regime that gave it safe harbor in Afghanistan, Rumsfeld got to take his theories out for a test drive. There, a small contingent of several hundred U.S. special ops troops and CIA operatives allied with local tribal militias relied on healthy doses of cash and precision air strikes to dislodge the Taliban from power in just a few months. It was initially a dramatic success, but the number of U.S. troops deployed to control the country reached 100,000 in 2011.

When the Bush administration's attention turned to Iraq in late 2002, Rumsfeld and his Army planners clashed anew. At first, Gen. Tommy Franks' war plan sounded like a reprise of the Desert Storm campaign of 1991, calling for a slow buildup of hundreds of thousands of troops in preparation for a large and decisive battle. The plan was a textbook continuation of the so-called Powell Doctrine, named after Colin Powell, the former Army general who was current Secretary of State. The Powell Doctrine held that the U.S. military should not be deployed unless clear risks to the nation's survival were at stake. And when committing troops, the war plans must emphasize overwhelming force, exit strategies, and when possible, broad support from the international community. Rumsfeld thought those policies were outdated, that the world's crises were too messy and

LIGHTNING MISSIONS
U.S. Army Rangers detained two Iraqi men in the city of Baqubah, 30 miles north of Baghdad, in 2003, after a predawn raid in which the Americans seized three municipal buildings to use as an operations center. The men were later released after the Rangers confiscated a small cache of arms.

too fast-moving and varied for such a rigid structure. Rumsfeld ordered Franks to throw out his Iraq war plan and focus on one that emphasized precision air strikes and small, nimble units that could decapitate the Iraqi regime before Saddam Hussein could even contemplate a counterstrategy. American and British forces ultimately deployed 170,000 troops (a third the number that participated in Desert Storm), and the drive to Baghdad was completed in just 21 days.

Special Forces played a central role in the Iraq campaign even before the war officially began. They slipped into the country, seizing airfields for the invading force and protecting oilfields from potential sabotage. They rolled into dozens of towns looking for arms caches, cleared mines from harbors and rivers, and hunted down top members of Saddam's regime.

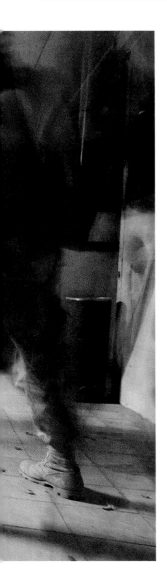

There was, of course, at least one crucial flaw in Rumsfeld's ambitious new way of warfare: He made no accommodations for occupation or reconstruction of newly conquered lands. If there is one thing special ops forces adamantly insist they are neither trained nor equipped to do, it is to hold and defend land. Without enough conventional forces to maintain law and order, both Afghanistan and Iraq slipped into states of insurgency and lawlessness—a situation that persists nearly a decade later.

Yet even as Iraq and Afghanistan were morphing into larger, lingering nightmares, the American military's transformation kept going. In 2003, Rumsfeld brought in Gen. Peter Schoomaker, who had been an original member

HE BAGGED BIN LADEN
McRaven, a former SEAL, became Special Ops chief.

of Delta Force and who had spent most of his career in special ops, to become the Army's Chief of Staff. The first time a Special Forces alumnus had been tapped as head of the entire Army, it was a watershed moment, as momentous as Stan McChrystal's appointment to a major combat command.

Rumsfeld began expanding the special ops budget and role as well. Against some admirals' resistance, for example, he supported the initiative to modify submarines to carry SEAL delivery vehicles in place of Trident nuclear missiles. And in 2004 he announced plans to bring home an additional 70,000 troops from the U.S.'s large Cold War–era bases in Asia and Europe, even as he expanded a network of smaller, more streamlined bases elsewhere around the world to support rotational units rather than permanently garrisoned ones.

During his tenure, Rumsfeld doubled the total special ops budget to $7 billion, and nowhere was the change more dramatic than the invigoration of JSOC. An executive order drawn up by Rumsfeld in 2004 and approved by President Bush identified up to 20 countries, including Syria, Pakistan, Yemen, and Saudi Arabia, that were believed to be harboring al Qaeda, and it gave JSOC broad authority to operate in those countries. With Rumsfeld's blessing, JSOC went from being an organization that merely provided forces to other commanders to a full-fledged war-fighting command, one that could operate independently of other U.S. military jurisdictions virtually anywhere in the world. In the name of fighting global terrorism, JSOC has become, effectively, an armed service unto itself.

Putting a Hit on Iraq's Most Wanted

Hibhib, Iraq, 2006

SYRIA

• Mosul

IRAN

JORDAN

IRAQ

Zarqawi killed in bomb blast

Hibhib •

Baghdad

Tigris R.

Euphrates R.

SAUDI ARABIA

Basra •

KUWAIT

The Mission

In the virtual civil war among rival factions in Iraq after the U.S. invasion, the rise of Abu Musab al-Zarqawi as the leader of al Qaeda in Iraq became particularly worrisome. The aim of the Jordanian-born radical was to drive out foreign forces and stir violence between his fellow Sunni Muslims and the country's Shi'ites. His methods: bombings, beheadings, and other terrorist tactics. The U.S. military put a $25 million bounty on him in its effort to track him down.

Capturing him became the focus of Task Force 145, comprising members of virtually every American special ops unit. It was organized into four geographic subcommands, each operating autonomously and at an unrelenting pace, launch-

ing at least a mission a day. Based on the intelligence that was gleaned in each raid, units would move on to a new mission within hours.

U.S. operatives tracking Sheik Abdul Rahman, a spiritual adviser to Zarqawi, determined that he switched transportation regularly but always used a particular blue car to visit Zarqawi. On June 7, 2006, a U.S. drone observed him getting into a blue car. A Delta Force team was dispatched to the site, a house in the village of Hibhib, about 55 miles north of Baghdad. But almost as soon as the commandos arrived, they feared they were going to lose their man. Their team was too small to raid the house on their own, but waiting for reinforcements might take too long. The team saw one group leave

the house. Zarqawi was not in the group, but special ops commanders decided they needed to call in conventional air power. Two Air Force F-16s were in the area and got the order to drop two laser-guided 500-pound bombs on the house. Rahman and several others were killed instantly; Zarqawi died of his injuries about an hour later and was identified by fingerprints and DNA comparisons. His death was the biggest U.S. manhunt victory since the capture of Saddam Hussein in 2003.

Over time, the special ops' ability to track down fugitives in Iraq improved dramatically. According to *Top Secret America*, by *Washington Post* journalists Dana Priest and William M. Arkin, "By 2004, the [National Security Agency] had figured out how to geolocate cellphones even if they were off. 'We just had a field day,' said a senior commander. 'We did thousands of them.' When they hit on a hot phone— 'the Find,' as they called it—someone would send a plane to watch the building where the phone had lit up, and a raid would be mounted if appropriate. Their surveillance fleet, a hodgepodge of 15 types of aircraft, grew from one aircraft to 40 in the matter of a year or so."

CHAPTER 6

The Killer Elite

WHILE DELTA FORCE IS best known today for its missions in the Middle East, the Army unit has deployed in hot spots all over the world. Operation Acid Gambit remains a classic example of a clandestine strike on foreign terrain: efficient, stealthy, deadly, quick—and capable of finishing successfully even after a setback. During the late 1980s, as Manuel Noriega's dictatorship in Panama reached new levels of brutality, an American citizen living in Panama City named Kurt Muse became a locus of the resistance movement when he began using a radio transmitter to broadcast anti-Noriega, pro-democracy messages. (Speculation had it that Muse was a CIA operative.) Apprehended while returning

HIGH PROFILE
The Navy's most elite group, SEAL Team 6, operated mostly in the shadows until its takedown of Osama bin Laden made it famous.

to Panama after a visit to the U.S. in March 1989, Muse was sent to the notorious Modelo Prison, where he languished, often beaten and often in isolation, for the next nine months.

As part of the larger U.S. military mission to invade Panama and depose Noriega, Delta Force was given the task of finding and rescuing Muse. Just after midnight on December 20, 1989, as the rest of the military began attacking Panama on multiple fronts, Delta sniper teams who had been inserted in the hills surrounding the prison shot and killed the complex's rooftop guards and then shot out the building's generator, plunging it into darkness, according to an account in *Night Stalkers*, by military writer Fred J. Pushies. At the same time, two AH-6 Little Bird light-attack helicopters began raking the surrounding buildings with machine guns to discourage any counterattack. Soon after the opening hail of fire, four more Little Birds dropped a Delta assault team of two dozen operators on the target building's roof. After blowing the roof door open with explosives, the night-vision-equipped soldiers swiftly navigated the stairs and corridors they had memorized during training, killing several guards who tried to oppose them. The operators found Muse's cell flanked by two guards. They killed one and bound the other after he immediately surrendered. After blowing open the cell door and handing Muse a helmet and flak jacket, they whisked him back up to the roof and trundled him into one of the returning Little Birds.

But they were far from in the clear. And what came next demonstrates a skill that special ops consider as important as sticking to a meticulously crafted plan: improvisation when a plan falls apart. After ducking a power line, the Little Bird carrying Muse was struck by Panamanian gunfire and forced to crash-land, injuring three of the five operators escorting Muse. The soldiers, two pilots, and Muse evacuated to a nearby building. Using their infrared beacons, they signaled their location to one of the other Little Birds, which relayed that location to a regular Army unit nearby, which picked them up in an armored personnel carrier. Even with a downed helicopter, the Delta team had accomplished its mis-

THE SECRET ARMY
Delta Force operators, and the Army special ops troops who support them, work to fight terrorism, rescue hostages, and conduct raids.

sion and proved its competence in one of its core areas of expertise: hostage rescue.

A successful special ops mission requires a wide range of specialties and support units: intelligence, logistics, equipment, and supplies. But there is no factor more important than the men on the ground, the highly trained specialists who put their lives at risk and pull

the triggers to rescue hostages like Kurt Muse or take down terror targets like Osama bin Laden and other al Qaeda operatives. Within the most secret circles of the special forces are three units who spend the most time on the front lines and in combat: the Army's Delta Force, the Navy's SEAL Team 6, and the Air Force's 24th Special Tactics Squadron.

Founded in 1977 by Charlie Beckwith as the American answer to Britain's Special Air Service (SAS), Delta Force is the Army's most specialized and elite unit. Its primary focus is terrorist threats, hostage rescue, and unconventional warfare. Blurring the line between soldier and spy, they are specialists in covert action, sniping, and working behind enemy lines. Through

Tools of the Trade

To get their jobs done, special ops forces need special gear, almost always modified to suit their extraordinary tasks.

The AC-130 gunship is used by Air Force Special Ops for bombing raids and close air support.

The Mark II has been a classic since Vietnam.

The Chinook is the draft horse of military helicopters, carrying troops, supplies, and heavy equipment.

The M67 fragmentation hand grenade is lethal within a 15-foot radius.

This desert vehicle has a complex communications and weapons system.

The Black Hawk is the most versatile and most often modified of military helicopters.

Night-vision scopes pick up radiation not usually visible to the human eye.

The INVISIO Q7 headset features the latest in bone-conduction technology.

The Sig Sauer P226 pistol, used by SEALs since the 1980s, has a high-capacity clip.

Snipers depend on the M110 semiautomatic rifle for distant and difficult targets.

their rigorous training, they master a wide variety of such skills as breaching buildings through both stealth and force (they know when to pick a lock and when to simply blow a door open), high-performance driving, intelligence gathering, and surveillance. The philosophy of Delta's effectiveness is: speed, surprise, and lethality of action.

That last part is crucially important, and lethality is best ensured through accurate shooting. Delta operators are simply some of the best shots in the world. They practice shooting not just from standing, kneeling, and prone positions, but while walking and running and using a variety of firearms. In his book *Inside Delta Force*, retired Command Sgt. Maj. Eric L. Haney, who served on the first Delta detachment, described the painful blisters that Delta Force members developed on their shooting hands, which eventually hardened into callouses from practicing with powerful .45 caliber pistols eight hours a day, days on end. That degree of weapons practice is unheard of in the conventional Army, even among infantry troops.

Delta Force was set up to mimic the SAS, and that structure remains generally intact to this day. Delta Force comprises three squadrons, labeled A, B, and C. Each squadron has two or three sub-units known as "troops" (one sniper troop plus one or two assault troops). Each troop is made up of four or five teams of four men each. The modular team is the bedrock organizational element of Delta Force and its greatest difference from conventional Army forces. Unlike a regular Army infantry four- or five-man "fire team," which is designed to operate independently from the rest of its squad or platoon only for very short periods, Delta's four-man teams are trained to operate on their own for extended periods when necessary.

Founded in 1962, the Navy's SEAL program was designed to give the Navy a comprehensive amphibious commando unit. (SEAL stands for Sea, Air, and Land.) Throughout the Vietnam war, the Navy fielded two SEAL teams, numbers 1 and 2, both of which fought with great distinction. The Vietnam-era SEAL teams specialized in classic small-unit strikes, similar to the U.S. Army Rangers, but with a maritime focus. Each SEAL Team consisted of about 150 men, divided into 10 to 12 platoons of 14 men each, along with a

headquarters and support staff. A SEAL platoon is made up of two seven-man boat crews. That basic seven-man building block has never changed because the SEALs' most basic method of transport is the IBS (inflatable boat: small), which can be dropped from an airplane or a helicopter, launched from a boat, or jettisoned from a submarine.

Although they could parachute and perform purely land-based operations, SEALs cultivated a particular expertise in amphibious landings and scuba assaults; they excelled at underwater demolition and small-assault-craft operation. But they were also masters of stealth: One SEAL platoon started wearing the same sandals as the Viet Cong so that their footprints would be harder to track. Indeed, even though SEAL Teams 1 and 2 were secret upon their founding, interservice rivalry dragged them into the public light. Piqued at all the attention the Green Berets were getting, the Navy put the SEALs on a publicity tour in 1967.

In the aftermath of Operation Eagle Claw's disaster in the Iranian desert in 1980, Navy Lt. Cdr. Richard Marcinko, former commander of SEAL Team 2, insisted that a large SEAL unit devoted to counterterrorism should be one of the cornerstones of a joint Special Forces command. No such SEAL team existed yet, so Marcinko created one, a group of 75 enlisted men and 15 officers, which he stood up in less than a year. He called it SEAL Team 6. Why not SEAL Team 3? Because, he writes in his memoir, *Rogue Warrior*, "the number would make the Soviets believe that there were five other SEAL teams somewhere when there were really only two. Doom on you, Russkies." (There are believed to be 12 SEAL teams in total today.)

Like Delta, SEAL Team 6's primary responsibility is counterterrorism, but it has a special focus on maritime operations, including ship-borne hostages and the capture or defense of oil platforms or other coastal structures. Under Marcinko, SEAL Team 6 developed a reputation for being highly skilled but undisciplined. SEAL Team 6 has slowly shed that reputation, adopting a culture of cool, understated competence that is now the special ops ideal. SEAL expertise has expanded dramatically over the years; many of their missions have nothing to do with the

sea, notably the thousands of missions they have completed in Afghanistan and Iraq, as well as their famous raid that killed Osama bin Laden.

The Air Force's most elite unit, the 24th Special Tactics Squadron, has an exceedingly generic name, but the chances are that anytime Delta operators or SEAL Team 6 members are around, men from the 24th STS are there as well. The unit's patriarch is Col. John T. Carney Jr., who in 1977 saw the need for a small group of highly trained, on-the-ground air-traffic controllers who could penetrate deep beyond enemy lines and help direct U.S. attacks and aerial missions. These forces needed an advance recon group who could survey potential landing and bombing sites and install beacons, lights, and communications systems.

At first he scraped together a prototype team he called Brand X, numbering just six combat controllers, which he expanded into a full-fledged discipline and elite unit over the next 14 years. Today the 24th STS, which has seven squadrons, specializes in airfield seizures, controlling air strikes, and coordinating the movement of friendly ground forces out of harm's way. Embedded in its teams are highly trained medics called pararescue jumpers (or "PJs"), who specialize in retrieving and caring for hostages or special ops soldiers wounded in battle.

Since its inception, the 24th STS has been a part of virtually every well-known military conflict the U.S. has been engaged in, from Grenada and Panama to Iraq and Afghanistan. The 24th's fight for respect within the military has mirrored that of Delta Force and SEAL Team 6. As Carney wrote in his 2003 book, *No Room for Error*, just as the wars in Afghanistan and Iraq were becoming protracted conflicts, "Unlike previous forays where they had to beg for an invitation to get into the fight, at the turn of the 21st century America's military hierarchy looked to special tactics to win the day."

CHAPTER 7

Tinker, Tailor, Soldier, Spy

WHEN SADDAM HUSSEIN was found in his "spider hole" just outside Tikrit, Iraq, in December 2003, the 4th Infantry Division got almost all the media attention for rooting him out. That unit's soldiers dominated pretty much every photo op, but sometimes in the corners of those celebratory photos there would be a face or a uniform that had been digitally obscured by the Pentagon for security before releasing them to the media. Those blurry faces were the special ops forces who deserved much of the credit for tracking Saddam down. Some of the units who formed the Saddam-hunting team, dubbed Task Force 121, like the Army's Delta Force and Britain's SAS, are well known in lore and legend.

But one unit that played an integral role in Task Force 121 remains so low profile, and changes its name so often, that few people really know what it is called at any given time. Over the years it has gone by Centra Spike, Torn Victory, Capacity Gear, Task Force Orange, Robin Court, Grey Fox, and even the Secret Army of Northern Virginia. For expediency's sake, most black-op experts call it the Intelligence Support Activity (or ISA or simply "the Activity"). Founded in 1980, during an era when the CIA and the rest of the U.S. intelligence apparatus did not cooperate well with the military, the Activity is a U.S. Army unit designed to combine the most potent elements of civilian spycraft with the war-fighting capabilities of the military's other elite counterterrorism units. Since its founding, the Activity has played a role in virtually every U.S. military engagement, including the invasions of Panama, Afghanistan, and Iraq, as well as scores of secret operations, like the

track-down of Colombian drug lords and Serbian war criminals. Yet the Activity's exploits remain virtually unknown. British journalist Michael Smith's book *Killer Elite* is one of the only credible, authoritative accounts of the shadowy unit's history and current tactics, which have become key to U.S. war efforts in Afghanistan, Iraq, and beyond. "For much of its history the Activity has been about silent preparation of the battlefield ...," writes Smith, "but now the Activity finds itself in the lead role of a very proactive U.S. counterterrorist program that seeks out America's enemies with the express intention of 'fixing and finishing' them."

Starting before the invasion of Iraq, the Activity was among the handful of agencies taking the lead in tracking down high-ranking members of the Saddam regime. The Activity employed one of its specialties: signal intelligence. The Activity's operators eavesdropped on cellphone and sat-phone calls, tapped into Iraqi fiber-optic communications systems, and intercepted two-way radio transmissions between Saddam loyalists. After the regime had fallen and Saddam's ever-decreasing circle became more mindful of the dangers of electronic communication, the Activity and the CIA increasingly relied on human intelligence to tighten the noose. A pattern was soon established: Operators from Task Force 121 would raid a stronghold of suspected Saddam sympathizers; an intense interrogation of those detainees would result in a new round of leads, and Task Force troopers would mount a new sweep based on the intelligence almost immediately. By repeating that cycle with exhaustive frequency, Task Force 121 learned that Saddam was hiding out near his tribal homeland of Tikrit and traveling between more than a dozen safe houses in a beat-up Iraqi taxi, which are unvaryingly Toyota Corollas painted orange and white. Finally, on December 13, 2003, a detainee offered up fresh details on exactly where Saddam was—including the tidbit that he had an underground bunker—and a combined group of Task Force 121 and the 4th Infantry Division moved in.

Like many of the nation's most elite special ops units, the Intelligence Support Activity was born from frustration. Col. Jerry King was one of the founding fa-

thers of modern-day U.S. special ops and had been involved in Operation Eagle Claw, the failed hostage-rescue mission in Iran in 1980. While others focused on the helicopter pilots who hadn't been trained for the job and other such snafus, King, who was chief of staff to the Army general in charge of the operation, was appalled at the poor quality of intelligence that the CIA provided to the military. Although the spy agency offered up thousands of photos captured by satellites and SR-71 Blackbird spy planes, it claimed throughout the months of preparation not to have a single contactable agent or informant in the country.

Only days before the mission, the CIA turned over a trove of detailed intelligence that proved otherwise, in detail right down to the orientation of window latches inside the U.S. embassy building where American hostages were being held. King suspected that the CIA had possessed that information all along, but had figured that the rescue mission would never actually launch and was thus reluctant to give up its data and, in its view, needlessly compromise its source. Only when it became clear that Operation Eagle Claw was a go, King suspected, did the CIA pass along the bonanza it had been sitting on. To King, the CIA's duplicity was an intolerable offense that demonstrated that the CIA could not be trusted by its colleagues in uniform and that the military would have to create a full-fledged spy agency of its own. As plans spun up immediately in the aftermath of Eagle Claw to mount another rescue mission, King's boss handed him the task of forming a small team that could gather intelligence and infiltrate an advance team directly into Tehran without the CIA's help.

Recruiting heavily from Army Special Forces (of which he was a veteran), King called this early unit the Field Operations Group, or FOG. He liked the name, he

PARACHUTE PIONEERS
The Activity founder, Col. Jerry King (second from left), with colleagues during practice for a high-altitude jump

said, because it brought to mind the "hazy, ever-changing, hard to get a grip on, and often unpredictable."

FOG and the rest of the fledgling special ops units never had a chance to make their second rescue attempt; Tehran released the 52 U.S. hostages on January 20, 1981 as part of a deal brokered by the incoming Reagan administration, but King and many colleagues were committed to building up a military alternative to the CIA. Even William Casey, the new director of the CIA, agreed, believing that since it had a distinctly military focus, it should remain under military control. In March 1981, FOG was renamed the Intelligence Support Activity, and Col. Jerry King its first commander.

With a brief to provide intelligence to other special ops units, but also to possess offensive-warfighting capabilities of its own, the Activity, as it quickly became known, had no real precedent. Part spooks, part commandos. Unlike Delta and SEAL Team 6, it invested heavily in "signal intelligence" capabilities, machines that could eavesdrop on telephone conversations, two-way radio communiqués, and later cellphone and GPS signals. These operators were known as the "knob turners" for their propensity to sit hunched over in front of rows and rows of electronic dials as they tried to pluck just the right frequency out of the ether. One of the knob turners' earliest successes was in late 1981, when U.S. Army Gen. James Lee Dozier, who was working for NATO's southern command in Verona, Italy, was abducted from his home by the Red Brigades, a quasi-communist terrorist organization. The knob turners, flying over Verona in a Bell UH-1 "Huey" helicopter outfitted with the latest frequency-targeting equipment, slowly homed in on walkie-talkie handsets the Red Brigades were using. Ground units were then able to tail the kidnappers as they shuttled among their safe houses. The ISA passed the pinpoint location of Dozier to the Italian special police, who freed Dozier and arrested five Red Brigades members without a shot being fired.

The Activity is no mere geek outfit, however; it also specializes in the highly dangerous, on-the-ground covert fieldwork one usually associates with John Le Carre and Robert Ludlum novels. The Activity primarily recruits agents from the Army, but unlike most other special ops units, the Activity wants not just the best of the best in terms of physical fitness and technical proficiency, but actively seeks ethnic minorities from the Middle East, Latin America, and Asia. It prizes language skills and gives preference to those with training in electronics, computer programming, or psychological warfare. Unlike Delta and SEAL Team 6, women operators have been important to the Activity's work because they have frequently proved to be as good as or better than their male counterparts at intelligence gathering.

But Activity members are also proficient stealth warriors, trained in parachuting, survival, and evasion techniques, high-speed driving, and expert marksmanship with a variety of weapons. According to Smith's history of the Activity, the ISA pioneered the HAHO (high altitude, high opening) parachute technique for inserting troops stealthily into enemy territory and showed it to Delta Force.

With their multidimensional expertise and exceedingly low profile, the Activity was uniquely qualified to perform missions where the line between military action and law enforcement was blurry. Its existence was still a secret to Congress, for example, when the Reagan administration directed the Activity to feed El Salvadoran President José Napoleón Duarte with information it was collecting on the FMLN guerrilla group that was attempting to overthrow him. The Activity lurked in this murky shadowlands for decades, helping to take down Latin American drug kingpins such as Pablo Escobar (the ISA tracked him down via his cellphone) and apprehending Serbian war criminals throughout the 1980s and 1990s.

Since the 1991 Gulf War, relations between the military and the CIA have improved dramatically, to the point of a virtually equal partnership. When it came to hunting down Osama bin Laden, writes Smith in *Killer Elite*, "All the petty rivalries that hampered previous U.S. intelligence operations were put aside," to the degree that the entire operation was coordinated by the CIA. A key prospect was a courier who had once worked for bin Laden. "That's why the Activity's Pashtu-speaking 'knob turners' were listening in on [his] cellphone, waiting for him to make a mistake," according to Smith. "He only rarely turned his phone on, removing the battery to prevent the Activity reaching inside it to switch it back on, a technique they'd deployed to good effect before. When he did use it, he spoke only in predetermined code words." The courier finally tripped up when an old friend called one day and the courier told him, revealingly, "I'm back with

When the CIA Takes Up Arms

LESS THAN THREE MONTHS after the 9/11 attacks, Johnny "Mike" Spann, a paramilitary officer for the CIA, was interviewing prisoners at a 19th-century prison fortress outside Mazar-i-Sharif, Afghanistan. Instead of interviewing them one by one, Spann and his partner met with them as a group, trying to flesh out their links to al Qaeda. When a group of prisoners massed around Spann, he killed one with his pistol, and the prisoners swarmed, clawing at him with their bare hands. Spann killed two more before collapsing under the throng. He was the first American killed in action in the war on terror.

A descendant of America's covert operations during World War II, the CIA's Special Activities Division (SAD) was active throughout the Cold War in coups and paramilitary actions, with mixed results. The disastrous 1961 Bay of Pigs invasion in Cuba was one. SAD was active in dozens of coups, notably in Central America in the 1980s, as President Reagan sought to push back communism.

SAD recruits many of its officers from the

the people I was with before." The Activity was then sure they had found the man known as High Value Target No. 1. "All they had to do was wrap him in a cocoon of electronic, physical, and aerial surveillance and let him take them to the al Qaeda leader," Smith wrote.

When SEAL Team 6's shooters rode into Pakistan to take down bin Laden, riding on the choppers with them were Activity operators who uncovered what a senior intelligence official described as a "treasure trove of information," including five computers and bin Laden's handwritten journal. And the fact that almost no one has ever heard of the Activity, even though they fight alongside the Rangers, Delta Force, and SEAL Team 6? They prefer it that way.

military, particularly special ops, who undergo a yearlong training course at the CIA's training center at Camp Peary, Va., known as "the Farm."

Officers from SAD had been sneaking into Afghanistan for years to recruit spies for the agency. Before U.S. commandos entered the country after 9/11, SAD officers were already there organizing a paramilitary force to fight the Taliban. SAD officers entered the country in late September 2001 on a Soviet-made Mi-17 helicopter with weapons and a reported $3 million in cash to organize the Afghan warlords to fight alongside U.S. special ops forces. Among the SAD officers arriving on the scene was a 71-year-old former Green Beret, Billy Waugh, whose Vietnam decorations included a Silver Star, four Bronze Stars, and eight Purple Hearts. "Sometimes the boys from the agency don't agree with the lads from the [special forces]," Waugh says. "I kept the peace in that particular area." Even as the two sides get along, the competitive rivalry endures. "The agency doesn't share all its information with the Special Forces, and the Special Forces doesn't share all their information with the CIA," Waugh says. "Everybody has an ace in the hole they don't want to talk about." —*Nate Rawlings*

Bringing Down A Drug Kingpin

Medellín, Colombia, 1993

Advised by U.S. special ops, Colombian police chased the fleeing Escobar across rooftops and shot him dead.

The Mission

In the late 1980s Colombian cocaine lord Pablo Escobar had become a threat to his country's stability, so the U.S. resolved to help the Bogotá government capture or kill the billionaire fugitive. The challenge for U.S. special ops was to track him down in a land where many citizens viewed him as a kind of Robin Hood.

Not long after antidrug presidential candidate Luis Galán was killed in 1989—Escobar was suspected of ordering the hit—George Bush declared war on the drug cartels. Then, aiming at another candidate,

Escobar blew up Avianca Flight 203, killing 110 others instead, among them two Americans.

The U.S. responded by assigning the Army's Intelligence Support Activity, known as the Activity, to do the spywork necessary to take down Escobar. The Activity's operators used listening devices mounted on Beechcraft airplanes, picking up the drug lord's mobile-phone and shortwave messages. In 1990 the Activity learned of a plan by Escobar to assassinate yet another presidential candidate and told Colombian authorities. Security was beefed

up for all candidates, but a 16-year-old assassin managed to kill Bernardo Jaramillo. The Colombians accused Escobar, who denied it; the Colombians then reported as proof that the U.S. had used listening devices, blowing the Activity's cover and hampering its work.

President César Gaviria, in an attempt at rapprochement, agreed not to extradite Escobar to the U.S. if he turned himself in. Escobar did and ended up in La Catedral, a spacious compound that became his luxury prison. In 1992, when the government tried to move Escobar to anoth-

er facility, he escaped. The hunt resumed, and Gaviria created a special ops unit of his own, called Bloque de Búsqueda, or Search Bloc, backed by U.S. members of the Activity as well as Delta Force troops and Navy SEALs.

In late 1993 operatives picked up a signal that Escobar was in a middle-class section of Medellín. The Activity pinpointed the exact house. A 17-man assault force went in. Escobar was killed as he tried to flee across rooftops. His body had a bullet through the ear. Officially, at least, Escobar was taken down by Bloque de Búsquedas.

CHAPTER 8

Birds Of Prey

SPECIAL WARFARE OPERA-
tors prefer to do their work
in the shadows. It is not an
accident that their uniforms,
insignia—even their unit's
names—are obscure and con-
stantly changing. But if there is one highly visible icon
of fighting wars the special ops way, it's the MH-6
Little Bird helicopter bristling with an armed array of
commandos all but hanging off its sides as it swoops to
unload them in a pinpoint touchdown that lasts only
a few seconds before the tiny chopper zings off again
like a startled dragonfly.

Light and nimble, with room only for a pilot and
a co-pilot inside its capsule cockpit, the Little Bird was
originally designed as a Vietnam-era scout helicopter.
But America's counterterrorism forces, which needed

an agile craft to carry them low, fast, and undetected
across urban landscapes, jury-rigged the MH-6 into
an extraordinarily effective small-unit assault vehicle
by strapping some benches to its exterior.

As the Little Bird darts and dodges through hostile fire, up to six soldiers sit on the benches, often
with no restraint other than perhaps a light tether and
locking their ankles together. To fly this helicopter to
the edge of its capabilities—in a way it was distinctly
not designed to perform—takes a special kind of pilot,
a pilot who's every bit the commando that his passengers are.

Since they go everywhere, special ops forces have a
wide variety of transportation needs, not just the ones
at which Little Birds excel. Sometimes soldiers need
to be dropped off on a rooftop in a crowded city. Other
times they need to be carted deep into enemy territory
under the cover of darkness and as silently as possible.
While the U.S. military abounds in skilled pilots flying

SOARING
With two Night Stalkers at the controls, Rangers hang on tight to a Little Bird, waiting for it to reach the target so that they can jump off and get to work.

a wide range of aircraft, only one aviation unit has the explicit mandate to carry the likes of Delta Force, SEAL Team 6, and other elite units: the helicopter jockeys known as the Night Stalkers—or more officially the Army's 160th Special Operations Aviation Regiment (SOAR), based at Fort Campbell, Ky.

Like many special ops units, the creation of the Night Stalkers goes back to the lessons learned during Operation Eagle Claw, the ill-fated 1980 mission intended to rescue American hostages held by Iranian revolutionaries in Tehran. The pilots assigned to ferry the Delta operators into Iran were ill-suited to the task. Not that it was their fault: the RH-53D Sea Stallion helicopters pressed into service were heavy, lumbering mine-sweepers, and while the Marine Corps crews who flew them off the deck of the U.S.S. *Nimitz* were well accustomed to open-water flight and aircraft-carrier landings, they had little experience flying in the dark at low altitudes and into a howling sandstorm the way this mission required.

In fact, no helicopter unit in the Marine Corps, Air Force, or Army had much experience with that kind of aggressive, highly technical, and extremely dangerous flying. To rectify this weakness, the Army founded Task Force 160, a group of Black Hawk chopper pilots from the 101st Airborne Division who were given orders to transform themselves into a helicopter squadron that could pioneer a new mode of flight tailored to the needs of America's emerging counterterrorism specialists.

From the very beginning, the Night Stalkers have had an intimate relationship with the operators they carry. Many of the early pilots were former infantrymen with ground combat experience. One of the legends of the regiment, Michael Grimm, led an infantry platoon in Vietnam, where he earned the Distinguished Service Cross as well as several other awards for valor. Grimm became an aviator, and after another combat tour as a helicopter pilot, he became one of the first Night Stalker pilots. Bryan Brown, a Special Forces veteran, commanded the Night Stalkers and then rose to become the commander of JSOC. Night Stalker pilots now include former Rangers and other special ops alumni.

Today the 160th SOAR is a full combat squadron boasting the world's best helicopter pilots. As their nickname suggests, they pioneered fast, low, "nap of the earth" flying in the dark using night-vision goggles back when the technology was experimental. This expertise was hard bought and had to be learned first-hand, essentially through trial and error.

In the early days there was plenty of error. Between March and October 1983, for example, the Night Stalkers lost four helicopters and 16 personnel in training accidents. One commander began teaching a safety course called "How Do You Keep a Hangar From Being Named After You?" But over the years the 160th made good on its motto, "Night Stalkers don't quit," developing skills far beyond what was known a generation ago.

While nighttime combat operations remain its hallmark ("Death waits in the dark" is another motto), the 160th today excels at multiple forms of precision flying. The unit participated in the invasions of Grenada and Panama, and in 1988 Night Stalker pilots carried out their first night combat engagement, the special ops attack on the *Iran Ajr*, an Iranian ship that had been laying mines in the Persian Gulf during the Iran-Iraq war, posing a threat to U.S.-flagged cargo ships passing through the region.

Since then Night Stalkers have been a part of virtually every military engagement in which the U.S. has been involved, both the famous and the still unknown. In October 1993, Night Stalker helicopters flew in the battle of Mogadishu, during which two Black Hawks were shot down and five Night Stalkers (out of 18 U.S. casualties) were killed. Choppers from the 160th were among the first on the scene to both Afghanistan and Iraq. By 2005 the 160th had grown into a full regiment comprising three air battalions. They are the only Army aviation group that refuels aerially, extending the theoretical range of their battle groups around the world. They've become so proficient that they even have a performance guarantee for any unit

LOOKING FOR TROUBLE
U.S. Army Spc. Nicholas Miller of SOAR scans the Gulf of Mexico in a Chinook while on a tactical exercise.

they work with: They vow to be on target and on time, every time, plus or minus 30 seconds.

Helicopter pilots who want to join the Night Stalkers must first pass a stringent review of their experience, as well as a rigorous interview. Pilots invited to try out enter a weeks-long assessment phase during which they are given a series of intensive physical and flying challenges in which applicants are not told their target criteria or their scores upon completion. Screeners are always on the lookout for maturity and stress management. During one test, for example, the applicants receive a long list of tasks and are graded based on how they evaluate, prioritize, and complete them without any outside input. Pilots are likewise given a full psychological evaluation and a formal board review before a panel of senior officers.

Pilots who pass all those assessment tests are invited to join the Green Platoon, a testing and train-

ing phase that can last five to eight months. Pilots start with a three-week course on survival, escape, resistance, and evasion (SERE). They then move to combat skills and water survival training, including time in "the dunker," a full-scale cockpit crash simulator that plunges and rolls into a water tank as pilots and crews are trained how to escape a crashed and sinking aircraft. Next comes land navigation exercises, hand-to-hand combat training, and advanced personal weapons training.

Following that is four weeks of intensive flight instruction, including air-crew coordination, night-goggle navigation, and radar navigation in both simulators and real choppers. The pilots practice close-formation flying in complete darkness, carry out long-range navigation exercises, simulate crash and aerial-evasion maneuvers, and fly for several hours using only night vision. One crucial test is "un-

plugged" navigation. A pilot is given a map, a compass, and a stopwatch and told to fly with no other navigation aids to an objective point within a certain amount of time while upholding the Night Stalker guarantee of "plus or minus 30 seconds."

During the final phase of Night Stalker training, pilots are assigned their specialty craft for detailed training on the Little Bird, Black Hawk, or Chinook. After completing Green Platoon, a Night Stalker pilot is "Basic Mission Qualified," which allows him to fly on live missions as a co-pilot. But the training never ends. After a year or two more of training and mission rotations, an aviator becomes "Full Mission Qualified" and eligible to be chief pilot on missions. After three to five more years, a pilot can become a mission or squadron leader.

The helicopters flown by the Night Stalkers come in three sizes: small, medium, and large, in this ascending order: the Little Bird, the Black Hawk, and the Chinook.

The Boeing Little Bird weighs just 2,000 pounds and is 25 feet long, but has a top speed of 175 miles per hour and a range of more than 230 nautical miles. They

are so small they can fit on any standard Air Force cargo plane and can be prepped for a mission within 15 minutes. An accomplished Little Bird pilot is capable of navigating a cityscape just a few feet off the ground, at night, flying between buildings over extended periods. The unarmed MH-6 can carry up to six commandos into battle on its external benches, and the armed AH-6 is the only light assault helicopter in the Army's arsenal. The AH-6M can carry a variety of fearsome weapons systems, including two miniguns that can fire 2,000 or 4,000 rounds per minute at a range of 1,000 meters and two seven-shot rocket pods that can fire a variety of payloads including high explosives, rounds filled with thousands of barbed darts, illumination rounds, and incendiary white phosphorous.

The mainstay of the 160th's helicopter fleet is the Sikorsky Black Hawk, one of the world's most versatile and rugged military helicopters. A Black Hawk typically carries a crew of four (two pilots and two gunners) and up to 14 soldiers. It has an unrefueled range of 1,200 nautical miles and a cruising ground speed of 185 miles per hour. The Night Stalkers fly several different specially modified Black Hawks, like the MH-60K,

which features terrain-following radar, a laser range-finder, and a color weather-map generator.

The Black Hawk that crashed during the raid on Osama bin Laden's hideout in Pakistan included modifications not before seen, such as an odd rotor configuration and what appeared to be added panels and surface coatings. It has been widely speculated that those variations were noise-reduction and radar-evasion advancements.

The 160th also flies a more heavily armed Black Hawk called the Direct Action Penetrator, or MH-60L, which has stub wings that can carry a 30mm automatic cannon and rocket pods, making it formidable in its role as an armed escort or fire-support craft.

With its uncommon dual-rotor design and its massive size, the 160th's heavy-lift and cargo helicopter, the Boeing MH-47 Chinook, is one of the most distinctive helicopters in the air. Flying with a crew of five, the Chinook's primary use is moving soldiers, heavy equipment, and supplies. Its large interior bay, accessed via a tilting rear ramp, can carry 55 soldiers and all their equipment or a Humvee. Anything too large to fit in its hull can be carried (up to 26,000 pounds)

via a sling load supported by three external hooks.

Despite its lumbering look, the Chinook is surprisingly nimble, with a normal cruising speed of 137 miles per hour. And it's versatile, capable of landing on ship decks, in cities and in mountains, and as a mass-casualty evacuation vessel or a search-and-rescue bird. One of the Night Stalker Chinook pilots' more remarkable techniques is a Navy SEAL exfiltration maneuver known as "The Delta Queen." With its ramp extended, a Chinook will hover over open water to the point that the ramp is submerged and the helicopter's hull is taking on water. A group of SEALs operating in an inflatable raft known as a Zodiac will gun the outboard motor and drive with a *thwomp* straight into the Chinook's interior. With water cascading like a waterfall out its back, the Chinook then lifts up and takes off with its SEAL cargo intact.

Black Hawk Down: Heroism and Hubris

Mogadishu, Somalia, 1993

The Mission

Somalia was racked in the early 1990s by civil war and famine, which prompted the UN to launch a peacekeeping mission. The U.S. and other nations sent in troops to restore order and rebuild the country. A power struggle ensued with warlord Mohamed Farrah Aidid, who had declared himself President. In June 1993 his forces were suspected in an ambush that killed 24 Pakistani troops. The next day the UN passed a resolution essentially declaring war on him.

The hostilities escalated. In July a U.S.-led helicopter assault on a house where Aidid was believed to be hiding failed to find the warlord but killed dozens of Somalians and led to the beating deaths of four Western journalists by an angry mob. In August, Aidid's militia blew up a U.S. military vehicle, killing four soldiers.

The rising violence prompted President Clinton to send 160 special ops troops to Somalia to capture Aidid. Called Task Force Ranger, it included Rangers, Delta, and SEALs.

On Oct. 3, acting on reports that two of Aidid's top lieutenants were in central Mogadishu, the task force launched an operation with 19 aircraft, 12 vehicles, and more than 100 troops. "Bristling with grenades and ammo, gripping the steel of their automatic weapons, their hearts pounding under their flak jackets, they waited with a heady mix of hope and dread," wrote Mark Bowden in *Black Hawk Down*. "It was an audacious daylight thrust into Aidid's stronghold."

The mission went immediately awry when a Ranger attempting to rope down from a Black Hawk fell 70 feet and was severely injured. As military vehicles tried to reach him, Aidid's militia and armed civilians came on the scene, and fierce battles erupted. Two Black Hawk helicopters were shot down. Delta Force snipers Randy Shugart and Gary Gordon arrived to defend the crash scene and put up a furious fight before they were killed. Dozens of U.S. troops were trapped overnight, surrounded by thousands

ELITE TROOPS, GRAVELY OUTNUMBERED
From left: one of the two Black Hawks shot down in central Mogadishu; Somalis show off clothing said to be from fallen U.S. soldiers; Shugart and Gordon received posthumous Medals of Honor.

of armed Somalis. The next day a massive convoy of 100 vehicles entered the city to rescue the besieged troops. By the time the battle was over, 18 U.S. soldiers had been killed and dozens wounded, and hundreds of Somalis were dead. Somali citizens dragged the bodies of U.S. soldiers through the streets, adding to the American humiliation. Days later Clinton called for the withdrawal of U.S. troops from Somalia. Two months later Defense Secretary Les Aspin stepped down.

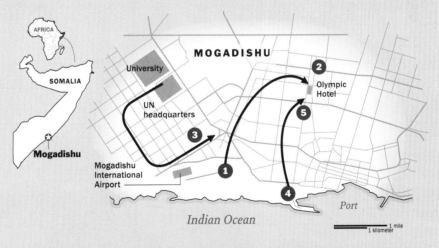

1. U.S. Rangers and Black Hawk helicopters raid a site near the Olympic Hotel.

2. After capturing 19 prisoners, the Americans are ambushed by Somali militia. Two U.S. helicopters are downed.

3. American relief forces in Humvees are ambushed by Somali forces near the K-4 traffic circle and retreat to the airport.

4. These troops join with Pakistani and Malaysian troops, but are delayed by logistical difficulties.

5. Relief finally reaches the U.S. forces more than nine hours after the assault started.

Post Op: How Do You Get A Life?

SPECIAL OPS SOLDIERS ARE highly perishable assets, not just because of the risk of injury or death, but because humans can function at such a demanding level for only so long. With a job that exceeds even pro athletes' in terms of physical and psychological stress, most commandos have only a few years of peak performance in them. Every operator secretly fears the day he becomes a step too slow, or his shots start veering an inch too wide. Eric Haney, a former Delta Force operator and author of *Inside Delta Force*, likens his own experience to "being an NFL player with no off season.... It just chewed people up." At some point every special ops soldier has to navigate not just pulling back from being a member of one of the world's most

elite fraternities, but leaving the military entirely.

Many special ops warriors manage to adapt quickly to the civilian workforce, given their skills and vigor. In general, hiring managers have long prized veterans as employees because they often demonstrate the discipline, teamwork, self-respect, and other virtues the military emphasizes. And those qualities are especially strong among special ops soldiers, a lot of whom move swiftly into corporate America, government, and law enforcement.

Many retired commandos find it difficult to leave the adrenaline rush of conflict zones behind for good, however, which is why a number of them transition to jobs with such defense-contracting security firms as Blackwater (now called Xe), Triple Canopy, and L-3, where they often find themselves back in action in Afghanistan and Iraq.

The popularity of defense-contracting jobs may be a symptom of a broader psychological phenomenon. Once you have been to war, it is hard to go back to a normal life. While that goes for many vets, special ops soldiers often find the change excruciatingly disorienting. In the summer of 2011, U.S. Army Special Forces Maj. Rusty Bradley had just finished a tour in Afghanistan organizing local militias. Before that, he had been commander of a Special Forces support company. Today he's nostalgic for the time he spent as a captain leading a Green Berets A-Team of 12 men on front-line operations through three tours of duty in Afghanistan, which he wrote about in the book *Lions of Kandahar.* "I don't really have the words to express it," he says about the day he had to relinquish command of his beloved A-Team, a group that had trained together and fought together under his command. "You train your whole life as a professional soldier to participate in something like this. When it's over, you wind up wondering, What do I do now? You spend the rest of your life wishing you were in command of something that good. It leaves you with a yearning because you know you will never experience anything like that again."

For special ops vets from elite units, those who have just come from the pinnacle of the military pyramid, the transition to civilian life is particularly jarring because their glory days are a secret. No one in the civilian world can appreciate the magnitude of the operator's service.

In some retirees' minds, says Howard Wasdin, a former SEAL Team 6 sniper and author of the bestseller named after his unit, "they've gone from rock stars to rock bottom. That's a tough pill to swallow."

Compounding some vets' difficult journey back to civilian life is the fact that the special ops community is lagging behind the rest of the military in taking seriously post-traumatic stress disorder (PTSD) as a normal response to combat, not as a weakness or a taboo subject. Wasdin says that for all the world-class training he had received, he got no counseling for either the undiagnosed PTSD he was suffering from or how to acclimate to a nonmilitary lifestyle. "I didn't realize I had post-traumatic stress disorder," he says. "I didn't realize I had survivor's guilt. I just thought that was a weakness being manifested because I wasn't man enough to suck it up. It would have helped more to downstage a little bit, instead of just getting your papers and saying, 'See you later.'" During the 1993 mission to Mogadishu, Somalia, known as the Black Hawk Down incident, Wasdin was shot three times and nearly lost his leg. Although he won the Silver Star for bravery, he could never return to full duty without pain and left the Navy in 1995. In the civilian world he seesawed between jobs, becoming a security team trainer, a cop, and a car salesman. Finally, after a chiropractor helped him with the shooting-related pain that had been nagging him for years, he trained to become a chiropractor himself and now has a practice in Jesup, Ga.

The life of a special ops soldier is notoriously hard on families. It is common for a Delta Force or SEAL Team 6 member to be deployed more than 220 days annually for years on end. Marriages frequently break up under the strain of such separations, or they survive the soldier's active-duty life yet fracture upon retirement, when long-buried resentments come to the fore. Rare

BACK FROM THE WILD
Howard Wasdin, author of SEAL Team Six, *suffered from PTSD after his service. Later he found a career as a chiropractor.*

is the former special operator's memoir that does not include some form of major marital discord. William Boykin was an original member of Delta Force who led a Delta squadron before commanding the entire organization. After hunting terrorists with a biblical fervor in Somalia and elsewhere, he ran afoul of the Bush administration for comments about his faith. Throughout his time in Delta Force, Boykin saw how a special ops career can pull a soldier away from his family. "You were gone a lot and your family very often didn't know where you were or how long you would be gone. And you could leave in the middle of the night, and in my case, maybe come home with a couple of holes in you. And I was not the only one. That was very, very stressful on families," Boykin says. "For the individual operator in Delta, it really was difficult to balance family life with the pressures, the needs, and the deployments associated with Delta. So we lost some guys as a result of it. They had

to choose—their wives literally gave them a choice—and some made the choice of Delta and lost their families. I'm divorced, and it was largely the result of the years of the kind of pressure that our marriage was under."

For author Wasdin, breaking the taboo about PTSD and the difficulties of juggling a family with a job that is far more than just a job were two of the reasons he decided to break the black-ops code of silence and write a book about his experiences, good and bad; one scene in Wasdin's book depicts him contemplating suicide. "I've gotten thousands of e-mails and letters saying, 'When I see that it's okay for you to say you have post-traumatic stress disorder and it bothered you, I feel okay asking for help now.'" But Wasdin's public profile is a rarity. Most retired special ops do not broadcast their former life. And if they used to be an operator for SEAL Team 6 or any of the secret units, they don't talk about it at all. You could be living next to one right now.

Warriors On the Screen

Time critic James Poniewozik looks at how special ops stories target audiences' hearts and minds.

THE ROLE OF SPECIAL OPS characters in Hollywood is not much different from the role of special ops warriors in real life: to project themselves into secret places to target objectives that cannot be reached by more direct means. In pop culture that stronghold is the subconscious. If traditional war stories about open combat represent a country's public face, then stories about commandos and secret operations are a means of speaking the unspoken.

Special ops stories became popular after World War II in pulp tales like Jack Kirby and Stan Lee's Sgt. Fury comics for Marvel. Like many war stories of their time, they were celebratory, but things soon grew more complicated. Over just a few years in the 1960s, the multimedia evolution of the story of the Green Berets tracked the quick shift in attitudes toward war and toward the U.S. military.

Even as the themes of protest music were crossing over onto the pop charts, Sgt. Barry Sadler's "The Ballad of the Green Berets" (co-written by Robin Moore) became the No. 1 single for five weeks in 1966—an un-ironic paean to the courage of "America's best" before the Summer of Love and the Tet offensive. Just two years later a version of the song appeared in the John Wayne movie *The Green Berets* (based loosely on a 1965 bestselling book, also by Moore). But that movie—a pro-war, anticommunist story released on the Fourth of July—made its debut in a very different world. Casualties were escalating in Vietnam, protesters were being beaten at the Democratic National Convention in Chicago, and

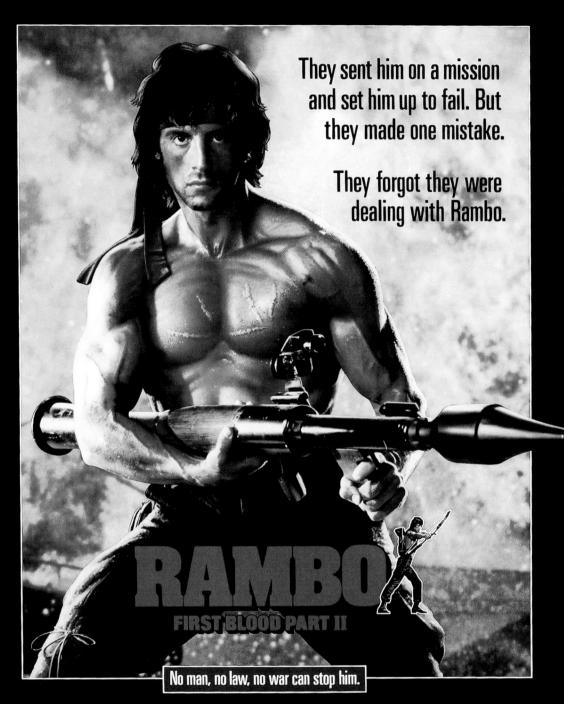

EVOLUTIONARY OPS
The Green Berets *(1968, top)* featured John Wayne as a super-patriot;
Apocalypse Now *(1979, right)* told a more harrowing tale of Vietnam; The Delta
Force *(1986, above)*, with Chuck Norris, had a happy ending to a hostage crisis.

the military was chafing at its restrictions in fighting the war. Wayne's glowing depiction of a soldier in a well-fought war, winning over a skeptical journalist and befriending a Vietnamese orphan boy, seemed less like drama torn from the headlines and more like wishful thinking.

Vietnam, however, cemented special ops as a modern prism through which to tell war stories. The conflict popularized the idea of a shadowy war with secret offensives and no front lines. As much as it was the "living room war," it was also unseeable and un-diagrammable in many of the ways in which we were accustomed to representing war.

When this new kind of war—fought in jungles and tunnels, not in trenches or on open fields—combined with the post-Watergate spirit of paranoia, war stories became about secret battles that exposed our subconscious minds. The 1979 film *Apocalypse Now* (based on Joseph Conrad's *Heart of Darkness*), with Marlon Brando as Col. Kurtz, the Special Forces officer who goes native (and goes mad) in the depths of the jungle, is nominally about Vietnam. More broadly, it's about corruption—moral and (with its images of gore and fetid rot) physical. As Kurtz is himself hunted by a covert operative, played by Martin Sheen, he becomes a symbol of a country that extended itself into a dark place and tapped a deep vein of ugliness.

But the unpopular war also contained the seeds for the special ops soldier as a different kind of hero: a poignant badass, used by his country and spurned by civilians, but strong and undefeated. In *First Blood* (based on a novel written while the Vietnam war was still being fought), Special Forces vet and former POW John Rambo (Sylvester Stallone) finds himself in America essentially fighting the war again, as a mission to find a friend (dead from Agent Orange) turns into a guerrilla fight against a corrupt sheriff's department. In the 1985 mega-hit sequel, the government frees Rambo from jail to send him to Vietnam to hunt for POWs.

Ironically, what is on the surface a thriller about government deceit (the feds are hoping Rambo will fail) became a symbol of post-Vietnam military resurgence. In Stallone's all-beef casing, Rambo embodied American power as a resurgent giant: He rises up to assert that there is no shame in his power and that

all he and his fellow vets want is "for our country to love us as much as we love it." Rambo was such a potent icon that in the Reagan '80s, he was claimed as a symbol by two political sides: To conservative admirers, he was American power recovering from its post-Vietnam guilt complex. To Reagan's opponents, he became shorthand for might-makes-right military arrogance and jingoism.

At the same time, TV was treating the spurned and vindicated special ops hero in a vehicle that was sillier and less controversial but arguably had as much cultural reach. *The A-Team*, on NBC, was more concerned with blowing things up than making statements, but at the heart of its premise was a story that was resonant in the post-Vietnam '80s: disposable heroes whom America used and then spurned. Accused, the prologue told us, of crimes they did not commit, Hannibal, B.A., and company took on explosive missions freelance; their country may have forsaken them, but they didn't forsake their country.

Throughout the '80s, special ops on screen gave America a chance to rewrite its recent military history. The second Rambo movie was a Southeast Asia do-over in which America was allowed to win. The campy 1986 action flick *The Delta Force*, starring Chuck Norris—later an outspoken Hollywood conservative— was set up as a kind of parable of military redemption from the Carter years. It opens on the disastrous 1980 attempt to rescue the hostages in Tehran by helicopter, with Maj. Scott McCoy (Norris) and Col. Nick Alexander (Lee Marvin) bemoaning their ill-use by Washington. "Why the hell wouldn't they listen, Nick?" McCoy asks. "We told them it's too dangerous to launch this operation at night." The colonel shakes his head: "They thought their plan was better." The movie climaxes with Delta Force saving a planeload of hostages in Beirut—doing it their way this time.

As time went on, special ops increasingly became the pop culture face of an era of quasi-wars and targeted operations. *Black Hawk Down*, the 1999 book

THE DIGITAL ERA
Left: The videogame Call of Duty enters a new chapter with Modern Warfare 3; Black Hawk Down *(top, 2001) resonated after 9/11;* The Bourne Ultimatum *(2007) starred a kinetic Matt Damon as a special ops vet.*

about a deadly raid on Mogadishu, Somalia, became shorthand for the nightmare scenario of an operation gone wrong, and a caution against the fantasy that special ops missions meant war could be fought with little cost or risk. But it was the Ridley Scott movie—a brilliantly disorienting welter of chaos—that captured the confusion of this new kind of war.

Black Hawk Down ended up being released in December 2001, a few months after the terror attacks that launched a new era of American battle: the long war, against stateless enemies, that had no treaty ceremonies or victory parades to look forward to.

After 9/11, special ops became the go-to means for depicting a war fought largely in the shadows; they simultaneously represented a fear (that our wars were being fought in secrecy and without accountability) and a fantasy (of highly competent, surgical warfare that was quick and efficient and killed only bad guys). TV's *The Unit*, co-created by playwright David Mamet, combined the action of Delta Force assignments

with the personal toll that the life took on soldiers' wives, stationed on base and often in the dark about their husbands' work. Characters from Jason Bourne (a former Delta Force member) to *24*'s Jack Bauer (a counterterrorist agent who had also been with Delta Force) showed us a war on terror that was both thrilling and, with the double- and triple-crosses of their plots, paranoid.

But they also made America's newest kind of war feel intensely intimate. This new war, their stories said, involved not only ruthlessness toward America's enemies, but sometimes toward its defenders. The signal defining scene of *24* comes at the end of season four, when Bauer, framed by his own government, fakes his own death and walks alone down a train track into hiding, having thanklessly saved the country once again.

The power of all these stories is that they're able to boil down complex geopolitical battles into one soldier, alone. Which is why maybe the most compelling and wide-reaching depictions of special ops today are not in movies or TV but in that 21st-century medium, the first-person-shooter videogame—like the Call of Duty series (*Modern Warfare* and *Black Ops*) and *Medal of Honor* (based on the Operation Anaconda mission in Afghanistan).

The games emphasize firepower over emotion, but they also do something that passively watching a screen can't: simulate the claustrophobic, chaotic sensations of battle (minus, of course, the threat of imminent death). And the perspectives they offer can be as controversial as any Hollywood movie: after public outrage over *Medal of Honor*'s multiplayer mode, which allowed players to fight as the Taliban, the game changed the name of the adversary to the generic "Opposing Force."

These first-person shooters' bleak battlescapes and moral ambiguity are a long way from John Wayne walking off into the sunset, promising to look out for a grateful Vietnamese boy. But in one way they show that, half a century later, the Special Forces still have the same distinct role in our war stories: focusing the narrative of vast conflicts onto small units. These soldiers don't just make war. They make it personal.

Photo Credits

Hawkeye, a black lab belonging to Navy SEAL Jon Tumilson, 35, of Rockford, Iowa, who was killed in the Aug. 6 helicopter crash in Afghanistan, was taken by his family to Tumilson's funeral, where he spent the entire service lying by the casket. A friend has since adopted the dog.